All You Wanted to Know About the U.K.

装幀 ● 菊地信義
装画 ● 野村俊夫

翻訳 ● 公庄さつき
挿画 ● 木脇哲治

Published by Kodansha International Ltd.,
17-14 Otowa 1-chome, Bunkyo-ku, Tokyo 112-8652.
No part of this publication may be reproduced
in any form or by any means without permission
in writing from the publisher.

First Edition 1999

ISBN4-7700-2487-8
99 00 01 02 10 9 8 7 6 5 4 3 2 1

「英国」おもしろ雑学事典
All You Wanted to Know About the U.K.

ジャイルズ・マリー

まえがき

国籍だけで人に対して先入観を持つのは、煙草を吸ったり酒を飲んだり爪を噛んだりするのと同じように、悪いとわかっていながらやめることのできない癖のようなものである。好むと好まざるにかかわらず、私たちは外国人に対して多少なりとも固定観念——すなわち単純すぎるイメージを抱いている。アメリカ人は1人残らず騒々しくて体の大きな熱血漢で、フランス人はセックスのことしか頭にない陰険な人間ばかりであり、日本人は薄笑いを浮かべながらぺこぺこ頭を下げるバーバリーに身を固めた観光客にすぎないといったように。

英国人はこのような固定観念の規模を広げることにひと役買ってきたように見える。ほかの国々は、典型的なドイツ人や典型的なイタリア人というように、人が型にはめられるだけですんでいるのに、英国の場合は社会全体が型にはめられている。

広く蔓延してある誤解によると、英国は確固たる階級制度によって形作られた国家であるという。ピラミッドの頂点に鎮座しているのは王室である。その下には上品な身なりをした“紳士”階級が位置しており、彼らは山高帽を頭に乗せてロールスロイスで外出し、妻たちはローラアシュレイのドレスに身を包み、バラの咲き乱れる庭園に座って、ウェッジウッドのティーカップからアールグレイの紅茶を飲んでいるという。そして社会の最下層には、パンクロッカーやサッカーフーリガンや失業者がひしめいている。

INTRODUCTION

Having preconceived ideas about people based on no more evidence than their nationality is a habit which, like smoking, drinking or biting one's nails, we all know to be bad, but, nonetheless, find difficult to give up. Like it or not, we all to some extent believe in national stereotypes—the over-simplified myths according to which all Americans are loud, large, and gung-ho, all Frenchmen sly and sex-obsessed, and the Japanese no more than grinning, bowing, Burberry-clad tourists.

The British seem to lend themselves to this kind of stereotyping on a big scale. While other countries escape relatively lightly with a stereotype of the individual—the typical German, the typical Italian—in Britain's case it is society in its entirety that is typecast.

Britain—goes the popular misconception—is organized in a rigid class system.The Royal Family sit at the apex of the pyramid. They are followed by a caste of exquisitely dressed "gentlemen" who—supposedly—spend their bowler-hatted days popping in and out of Rolls Royces, while their Laura Ashley-clad wives sit among the roses, drinking Earl Grey tea from fine Wedgewood china. At the bottom of this social heap, squirm the punk rockers, the soccer hooligans, and the unemployed.

　英国に関するこのような極端なイメージは、一方では
『モーリス』や『フォー・ウェディング』、他方では『トレインス
ポッティング』や『フル・モンティ』などの映画の影響による
ものだろう。そのなかには真実も含まれてはいるが、もち
ろんこれがすべてではない。

　一般に信じられている典型的な英国像が吟味に耐える
ものでないことは、少し考えてみれば明らかだ。事態は
それほど単純ではないのである。目を凝らして見れば、英
国社会が矛盾や自家撞着に満ち満ちていることがわかる
はずだ。たとえば、王室はたしかに目立つ存在ではある
が、あまり人気があるようには見えない。それに、ヨーロッ
パの他の国々よりもいよいよ貧しくなりつつある国家に、
どういうわけで上品な身なりの裕福な"紳士"が大挙して
存在し得るのか?

　本書は、英国をめぐる状況が一枚岩的なものではなく、
一般に考えられているよりも複雑で興味深いことを示すと
ともに、なぜ英国人はあんなにまずい食事をみずから進
んで食べるのか、学費が高くて簡単には入学できない学
校を"パブリックスクール"と呼ぶのはなぜなのかといった、
外国人なら誰でも不思議に思う英国に関する基本的で素
朴な疑問にも答えることを目指した。

　最後に、読みはじめる前に単純な言葉の問題を2、3指
摘させてもらいたい。本書は英国英語で執筆したため、
英国式の言葉遣いだということを覚えておいてほしいの
だ。映画は movie ではなく film であり、chips はフライド
ポテトで、ポテトチップは crisps と表記している。また、
イギリス人(English)という言葉はイングランドに住む人々
を差す場合のみに使用し(スコットランド人、ウェールズ人、
アイルランド人は指さない)、イギリス諸島に住む人々すべ
てを指す場合は英国人(British)という表現を使っている。

　　　　　　　　　　　　　　　　ジャイルズ・マリー

This polarised perception of Britain derives from films such as *Maurice* or *4 Weddings and a Funeral*, on the one hand, and *Trainspotting* and *The Full Monty* on the other. There is some truth in it, but not, by any means, the whole truth.

A little thought shows that the popular stereotypes just don't stand up to scrutiny. Things are just not that simple. If we look a little deeper, we can see that British society is full of paradoxes and contradictions. The royal family, for instance, is certainly prominent, but it hardly seems to be popular. And how can legions of rich and well-dressed "gentlemen" exist in a country that is becoming ever poorer than its European neighbours?

In addition to showing that things are far less monolithic, and much more complex and interesting than the popular preconceptions would have us believe, this book also aims to answer some of the basic and simple questions that any foreigner wants to ask about the UK. Why on earth should people voluntarily eat such disgusting food? Why should a school that is expensive and difficult to get into be called a "public" school?

Finally, a few simple language points before you start. Since this book is written in British English, be prepared for British usage. This means that a "movie" is a "film", "chips" are "French Fries", and "crisps" are "potato chips". Also notice that English is used to mean English people only (not Scots, Welsh or Irish), whereas British is used to refer to everyone in the British isles.

Giles Murray

目次

CONTENTS

文化

飲食

ENTERTAINMENT

FOOD & DRINK

娯楽・スポーツ

政治と王室

歴史

SPORTS

POLITICS & ROYALTY

HISTORY

経済

その他

ECONOMICS

MISCELLANY

性格

Q: 英国人とアメリカ人はどう違うのか？

アイルランド出身の才気あふれる劇作家、ジョージ・バーナード・ショーに、英国とアメリカは「共通の言語によって分断された2つの国家だ」という有名な警句がある。すなわち、言語を共有する英国人とアメリカ人は、よく似ていて理解し合えるはずだと思い込むために、似ても似つかないことに気づいたときには、言語が異なる場合よりも大きなショックを受けるというのである。

単純に肉体だけを見ても両者のあいだには違いが存在する。アメリカ人は英国人よりも背が高く、恰幅もよくて、かなり大柄だ。声もアメリカ人のほうが大きく、服装も派手である。医学的検査の結果明らかになったことだが、脳のなかのウィットやアイロニーを司る部分がアメリカ人には欠けており、そのためにアインシュタインのようなひと握りの人々を別にすれば、アメリカ人は英国人の繊細なユーモアを理解する能力を持たない。

行動様式も異なっている。英国人はきわめて内気で社交下手だが、アメリカ人はどこまでもあけっぴろげで、初対面の人にさえ、「やあ、元気？」などと大声で話しかける。英国人は、アメリカ人のそのような大仰さを“薄っぺらで無意味”と評したがる。英国人に無視されたときには、それは喜ばしいことだと理解することが大切である。なぜならその英国人は、あなたに対して現実に感じてもいない親しみを表すことによってあなたを欺こうとはしなかったのだから。

英国人はアメリカ人よりも厭世的で、なにごとにも否定的な態度をとる国民だ。お元気ですかと問われれば、アメリカ人なら「元気ですとも」と請け

Q: What are the differences between British and American people?

The Irish wit and playwright George Bernard Shaw famously remarked that England and America were "two countries divided by a common language." To explain the epigram: Because  both the British and American people share the same language, they assume that they are similar and will understand each other, so the greater their shock when they find themselves completely different.

Let's look at simple physical differences first. Americans are much bigger—both taller and bulkier—than the British. Their voices (and their clothes) are very much louder. Medical tests have also shown that the part of the brain that deals with wit and irony is physically absent from the American, rendering all but the most Einstein-like specimens incapable of understanding the subtleties of British humor.

Now let's move on to differences of behavior. While British people are very shy and socially awkward, Americans are uninhibitedly friendly, greeting even people they've never met before with a loud "How are you doing?" The British like to say that such effusiveness is "superficial and meaningless." When you are ignored by a British person then, it is important to understand that this is a good thing because he or she is not deceiving you by showing a warmth toward you he does not feel.

British people are more world-weary and negative than the Americans. If asked how they are, while the American may well declare that "he is doing good," or even "great," the

合うだろうし、ときには「絶好調ですよ」とさえ言う
かもしれないが、あくまで慎重な英国人は、「悪く
はないと言ったところでしょうかね」と答えてため
息をつくだろう。アメリカ人は英国人よりもはるか
に前向きで精力的だ。かつて私のガールフレンド
の母親が、アメリカ人は誰でも努力すれば大統領
になれると思いこんでいる、と言ったことがあっ
た。それに引き替え英国人は、なにをやってもそ
の努力が失敗に終わるようなある "仕組み" がこの
世には存在すると信じる傾向にあり、そのために
最初から無駄な努力はしないことに決めている。

英国人のこの活力の欠如がプラスに働いている
と言えそうな領域が1つ存在する。それは金を稼
ぎ、物質的な成功を手に入れることだ。アメリカ
では貧困は麻薬や銃、あるいは危険を意味するた
めに、アメリカ人は貧困を極度に恐れている。恐
怖心という否定的な動機に衝き動かされて、彼ら
は懸命に働くのだ。一方英国人は、恐れるものが
ほとんどなにもないために、野心を持たず、怠け
ていられるのである。

英国人とアメリカ人の関係は、アナロジーによ
って説明するのが一番かもしれない。アメリカ人
がつやつや光る果汁のたっぷり詰まった熟したプ
ラムの実だとすれば、私たち英国人は生きる歓び
を抜きとられたしなびたドライプルーンと言えるだ
ろう。

Q: "英国人の家はその城" と言われるのはなぜか?

英国人のマイホーム所有率は(たとえばフランス
の54パーセントと比較すると)きわめて高く、67パ
ーセントに達している。これは、地方自治体から
住居を賃貸している人々がその住居を購入できる
ようにして、"おんぶに抱っこ" の政府から脱却

cautious Briton will respond with a "not too bad, I suppose" accompanied by a sigh. The Americans are much more positive and dynamic than the British. I remember my girlfriend's mother telling me that people in the U.S.A. believed that anyone could become president if they tried. The British, by contrast, like to believe there is a "system" that dooms any action they take to failure, so they pre-emptively give up.

There is one area where this absence of vigor in the British may be a good thing. It is in the field of money-making and material success. Americans are terrified of poverty, because poverty in America is drugs, guns, and danger. Fear—a negative motivation—drives them to work hard. The British, by contrast, are unambitious and lazy because they have nothing much to be afraid of.

Perhaps the relation between British and Americans can best be explained by an analogy. If the Americans are fat, juicy, gleaming, plums, then we—the Brits—are shriveled, desiccated prunes, with all the natural *joie de vivre* sucked out of us.

Q: Why do they say "An Englishman's home is his castle?"

Home-ownership in Britian is extremely high at 67 percent (compared, say, to 54 percent in France). This is due partly to reforms in the Thatcher era (1979–90) which aimed to reduce the role of the "nanny state" by enabling tenants to buy the accommodation they were renting from the local council. There

しようとしたサッチャー政権時代（1979〜1990）の
改革の成果とも言えるだろう。ただし、その背景
に心理的な要素があるのも間違いないところだ。
"英国人の家はその城"という諺にも見られるよう
に、英国人に野心というものがもし1つでもあると
するなら、それはマイホームを持つことなのだか
ら。

　賃貸目的で建てられたマンション（英国では"フ
ラット"と呼ばれる）が英国で人気を博したことは
これまで一度もなく、賃貸住宅と言えば、地方自
治体が経費を抑えて猛スピードで建設した安普請
のマンションか、さもなければ19世紀のテラスハウ
スを不自然に分割した家と相場が決まっている。
しかも賃貸料がきわめて高いことから、コストパ
フォーマンスの点から考えても、ローンを組んでマ
イホームを買うのが一番なのだ。

　金融業界が好景気に沸き、ロンドンが世界金融
の中心地となったのをきっかけに、豪華マンショ
ンがまたぞろ建ちはじめたのは事実だ。しかし、
そういったマンションは、儲けすぎの株式ブロー
カーやトレーダー以外の人々には高嶺の花である。

　英国の建築様式は6つに分類することができる。
すなわち、チューダー様式（15世紀から16世紀）、
アン女王朝様式／ジョージ王朝様式（17世紀から
18世紀）、摂政時代様式（19世紀初頭）、ビクトリア
朝様式（19世紀後半）、エドワード7世様式（20世
紀初頭）、そしてそれ以外、の6つである。

　築20年を超えた家など古すぎてとても住めない
と日本人は考えるが、英国では金持ちほど古い家
に住みたがる。オアシスのリードシンガー、ノエ
ル・ギャラガーは億万長者で家を2軒所有してい
る。そのうち市中にある家は19世紀後半に建てら
れたもの（ビクトリア朝後期）で、田舎の別宅のほ
うはチューダー様式だ。

is, however, a psychological dimension. "An Englishman's house is his castle" goes the old saying, and if British people have one ambition, it is to own their own home.

Purpose-built apartments (known as flats in Britain) never really became popular in Britain, and rental accommodation is either jerry-built property erected at high-speed and low-cost by the local council, or awkwardly subdivided conversions of nineteenth-century terraced houses. Rents also tend to be very high, so in cost-performance terms buying a house with a mortgage is really the best option.

It must be noted that since the big boom in financial services made London a world-center, flashy apartments have started to be built again. They are, however, well out of the reach of any but the most overpaid broker or trader.

British architectural styles can be divided into six broad groups: Tudor (fifteenth/sixteenth century), Queen Anne/ Georgian (seventeenth/eighteenth century), Regency (early nineteenth century), Victorian (late nineteenth century), Edwardian (early twentieth century) and everything else.

The Japanese regard a property built twenty years ago as ancient and probably uninhabitable. In Britain, by contrast, the richer you are, the older the house you buy. Noel Gallagher, the lead singer of Oasis and a multimillionaire, has two houses. His town house dates from the late nineteenth century (late Victorian), while his country house is Tudor.

　マイホームへのこだわりにはマイナス面も存在
する。良質な住宅に住む人々は、そのままそこに
住みつづけたいと考えるため、なんの特徴もない
畳の部屋ではとうてい真似できないほど労働力の
流動性が低下する。居心地のいい家はまた、人を
満足させ、幸せにし、もっと一生懸命働こうという
意欲を減退させる。それに比べて日本では、どん
なに懸命に働いてもウサギ小屋のような家にしか
住むことができない。日本の経済が世界一活気が
あるのはそのせいなのである。

Q: 英国人は外国人をどう見ているか?

　英国人は外国人恐怖症を患っている。このこと
は、英国人が外国人を呼ぶときの侮蔑的なあだ名
からも明らかだ。あだ名をつけられた外国の大半
は、歴史上のいずれかの時点で英国と戦った敵国
である。ドイツ人は"クラウト"(キャベツの酢漬け
を意味するドイツ語の"ザウアークラウト"より)と
呼ばれ、フランス人はフランス革命が勃発した1789
年当時から、堕落したフランス貴族の贅沢な食生
活に言及した"蛙"というあだ名で呼ばれている。
　日本人がいまだに、英国人とはスーツに身をか
ためた紳士だと誤った思いこみを抱いているのと
同じように、英国人も外国人に対して相当に時代
遅れな固定観念を持っている。休暇で旅行に出る
英国人は、イタリアへ行ったらスリに遭う危険が高
いと考える。イタリアがまだ経済的に発展途上に
あった1950年代ならばそのような危惧も的を射て
いたかもしれないが、イタリアの国内総生産が英
国をしのいだいまとなっては、かえってイタリア人
のほうが、貧困にあえぐ英国人観光客から金を奪
われる心配をする資格があると言えるだろう。
　島国に住む英国人は、ヨーロッパ大陸に住む

This fetish for owning one's own house does have a negative side. People with nice houses tend to want to stay in them, so mobility of labor is reduced in a way that a nondescript *tatami* room could never achieve. A pleasant home also makes the resident happy and content, dimming his or her urge to work harder and harder. In Japan, by contrast, however hard you work, you always have to live like a battery-hen. Hence the world-beating vigor of the Japanese economy.

Q: How do the British regard foreigners?

The British are a xenophobic people. This is evident from the derogatory nicknames that they have for foreign nationalities, most of whom they have been at war with at some time in their history. The Germans are called the "Krauts" (from the German word "*sauerkraut*" or pickled cabbage), while the French are known as "Frogs"—a name which dates back all the way to the French Revolution in 1789 and refers to the luxurious eating habits of degenerate French aristocrats!

Just as the Japanese still mistakenly assume the British to be suit-clad gentlemen, the British, too, have rather out-of-date views of other nationalities. The British holiday-maker assumes that if he goes to Italy the chances that he will be pickpocketed are very high. This may have been true in the 1950s, when Italy was still economically underdeveloped, but now that it has a higher GDP than Britain, the Italians have more right to worry about being robbed by impoverished British tourists!

As islanders the British are far less accustomed to mixing

人々に比べて外国人とのつき合いに不慣れである。かつて大英帝国を築きあげた国民ゆえ、外国人に対して威張り散らすことには慣れていても、対等のつき合いは苦手なのだ。

もっとも、だからといって、英国人が外国人を特別に敵視していると考えるのは間違いである。英国人は自国民に対しても同じように敵意を抱き、疑心暗鬼にとらわれているのだから。スコットランド人は"ジョック"と呼ばれて嘲笑されているし、ウェールズ人は"タフ"と呼ばれ、アイルランド人は"パディ"や"ミック"とあだ名されている。疑い深く、他人となかなかうち解けることのできない英国人は、よそよそしい態度をとる口実として使えるものは、国籍であれ出身地であれ階級であれ、なんでも進んで利用しようとするのである。

Q: 英国人でもセックスをすることがあるのか？

ビクトリア朝時代、嫁いでいく若い娘に対して母親は、新婚初夜に新郎がことをいたしているあいだ「目をつぶってイングランド国家のことを考えなさい」と助言したという。

1940年代にハンガリー出身の作家ジョージ・ミケシュが、イギリス人の性格と習性に関するユーモアあふれる随筆を書いてベストセラーになった。ミケシュはその随筆のなかで、英国人のセックスについて、ここにその全文を掲載できるくらい短い1章を費やして述べている。

「ヨーロッパ大陸の人々には性生活があるが、イギリス人には湯たんぽがある」
"セックスお断り。我々は英国人です"というこのようなイメージは、社会が豊かになって移動が容易になり、避妊薬が開発されて人々の意識と行動

with foreigners than people in continental Europe. As former empire-builders they certainly were accustomed to bullying foreigners, but hardly to dealing with them on equal terms.

It is wrong, however, to think of the British as specially hostile to foreigners. They are just as hostile and suspicious toward their own people. Scottish people are derided as "Jocks," Welsh people as "Taffs," and the Irish as "Paddies" or "Micks." The British—suspicious and slow to befriend—are willing to use anything—nationality, region, class—as a pretext to be stand-offish.

Q: Do British people ever have sex?

The story goes that in Victorian times young brides were advised by their mothers to "shut their eyes and think of England" as their husbands went to work on them on their wedding night.

In the 1940s George Mikes, the Hungarian author of a best-selling humorous book on English character and customs, included a chapter about sex so short that I can quote it in full here.

"Continental people have sex life; the English have hot water bottles."

This "No Sex. Please. We're British" image predates the "Swinging Sixties" and the onset of the permissive society where ways of thinking and behaving were transformed by

が変わり、社会が寛容になった"飛んでる60年代"
以前のものである。詩人のフィリップ・ラーキンは
次の作品のなかで、セックスは1963年に"始まっ
た"となかば本気で言っているほどだ。

> 性交が始まったのは
> 1963年
> （ぼくにはちょっと遅すぎた）
> 『チャタレー夫人の恋人』解禁と
> ビートルズLP盤発売の中間

いまではミック・ジャガーのような英国の精力絶
倫男や、パッツィー・ケンジットのような英国版魔
性の女も存在するが、彼らは典型的な英国人とは
言いがたい。

英国という国家は、性に対して大人げないとそ
しりを受けてきた。英国人は性を自然なものとし
て受けとめずに、滑稽なものか、あるいは忌むべ
きものとして取り扱う。海辺のリゾート地で売られ
ているふざけた絵はがきと、タブロイド紙の見せ
かけの純潔主義のあいだを右往左往している英
国人の性意識は、フランス人や日本人よりも、むし
ろアメリカ人のそれに近いと言えるだろう。

国家レベルではなく個人レベルにおける英国人
の性意識とテクニックに関しては、みなさんが独自
に調査することをお勧めしたい。一つ私からアド
バイスさせていただくとすれば、それはビールとフ
ライドポテトという代わり映えのしない食生活のお
かげで実際の年齢以上に老け込みくたびれる前
の、若い英国人を選ぶことである。

Q: 英国人はなぜあれほど古い建物にこだわるのか？

英国人は不思議なほど古い建物が好きである。
金があればあるほど買う家は古くなる。一流企業

increased affluence, increased mobility, and the birth-control pill. In a semi-serious poem Philip Larkin even claimed that sex "began" in 1963:

> *Sexual intercourse began*
> *In nineteen sixty-three*
> *(Which was rather late for me)*
> *Between the end of the Chatterley ban*
> *And the Beatles' first LP.*

Now there are British studs—like Mick Jagger, and British *femmes fatales*, like Patsy Kensit, but they are hardly typical.

As a nation the British are often accused of having an immature attitude to sex. Rather than treat it as something natural, they treat it either as something funny or as something scandalous. They swing between the prurience of the seaside postcard and the fake puritanism of the tabloid newspaper, making them closer to the Americans than to the French or the Japanese.

Moving to the sexual attitudes and prowess of the British on an individual, rather than a national, level, I recommend that you carry out your own research. My only advice would be to chose someone young, whose body has not yet been prematurely aged and coarsened by a relentless diet of beer and chips.

Q: Why are the British so devoted to old buildings?

The British are absurdly fond of old buildings. The richer people are, the older the house they buy. Most prestigious busi-

の大半は、ロンドンのメイフェア地区に建つ18世紀の邸宅に本社をかまえている。しかし、だからと言って、英国人が古い建物を好むのは伝統を重んじるせいだと解釈するのは間違いだろう。古い建物が好きなのは、どちらかと言えば英国人建築家や建設業者の手になる新しい建物に対する、至極当然な恐怖心によるものである。

英国の都市建築の多くは、第2次世界大戦中にドイツ軍の爆撃を受けて甚大な被害を被った。そして、ドイツ空軍の攻撃を免れた建物は、戦後になってから不動産開発業者によって破壊されつくしたと言われている。政府による"おんぶに抱っこ"の政策が最高潮に達した1950年代から1960年代にかけて、都市計画者や建築家は、"普遍的移動性""空中通路""生活工場"などといったスローガンに、鼓舞されてというよりはむしろ憑かれて、英国の多くの都市から人間性を奪い去った。古いもの、美しいもの、人間に見合ったサイズのものはことごとく打ち壊され、代わりに無個性なコンクリートの巨大な塊が建てられた。家並みは一棟の高層ビルに置き換えられ、商店街は箱形のショッピングセンターにとって代わられた。街路そのものも、車のための高速道路やトンネルへと変わり、人間のほうは地下道や歩道橋、あるいは連絡通路へと追いやられた。

このような壮大な都市計画は、モデルとしては見栄えがよく、未来を予感させたかもしれない。しかし、現実には大失敗に終わった。建築技術は変わっても、人の心は変わらなかったのである。人々は帰属意識を持つことのできる、居住に耐えうる環境に暮らしたがっていた。

結局、新しい建築物の多くは、特定の人々のみにしか適さないことが明らかになった。すなわち、犯罪者である。ひったくりに最適な地下道や薄暗い

nesses have their headquarters in grand eighteenth-century houses in London's Mayfair district. It would be wrong, however, to assume that this fondness for the old stems from a love of tradition. It stems much more from a well-justified fear of anything new created by British architects and builders.

Many British cities were badly damaged by German bombing raids during World War II. After the war, it is often said, property developers took care of whatever the bombs of the Luftwaffe had missed! In the 1950s and 1960s—the heyday of the nanny state—town-planners and architects, not so much inspired, as crazed, by slogans like "universal mobility," "walkways in the sky," and "factories for living" dehumanized many British cities. Tearing down anything old, anything beautiful, or anything of human scale, they substituted gigantic lumps of featureless concrete. Rows of houses were replaced by single tower blocks. Streets of shops were replaced by a single bunker-like shopping center. Streets themselves were replaced by highways and tunnels for cars, while people were relegated to subways and overpasses, or walkways.

These grandiose schemes may have looked fine and futuristic as models. In reality, however, they were a disaster. Building technologies may have changed, but human nature had not. People still wanted to live in a livable environment with a sense of community.

It turned out that many of the buildings were suitable for one category of people only. Criminals. They loved the pedestrian subways and underlit stairways which were ideal for

階段、そして落書きにうってつけの長々と延びるコンクリートの壁は、犯罪者たちにおおいに愛された。

ビルの多くはまた、急ごしらえの安普請という英国の伝統工法にのっとって建てられた。マンションの薄い壁を通して隣の家の物音が筒抜けで、エレベーターはいつも壊れていた。1967年にローナン・ポイントの事故が起きると、現代建築に対する国民の幻滅は頂点に達した。ローナン・ポイントとは、ガス爆発が起きた22階建ての高層ビルである。手抜き工事のおかげでビルの片側がトランプの札を倒したように崩れ、3人の死者が出た。

謙虚になった建築家は、彼らの手になる建築物に住まなければならない住人の希望を、以前に比べれば多少は思いやるようになった。しかし残念なことに、心に深い傷を負った英国人は、新しい建物は古い建物よりも粗悪になるに違いないといまでも固く信じており、「迷信に囚われ、感傷的かつノスタルジックで、後ろ向きで硬直した」とノーマン・フォスターが評する態度を身につけるようになった。いまや建築家は景観保護法によって大幅に活動を制限されており、面白みのある建物はまず建てることができなくなった。

英国の有名建築家の多くは、クライアントがより金持ちで、一般市民も英国人ほど建築家を恐れていない海外において代表作を創ってきた。ノーマン・フォスターの手になる香港の香港上海銀行や、リチャード・ロジャースがデザインしたパリのポンピドー・センターがその例である。

Q: 英国人の人生観はなぜあれほど後ろ向きなのか？

英国人は集合的疲弊状態におちいっている。産業革命、大英帝国の建設、2度にわたる世界大戦といった数世紀にまたがる苦難が、かつては活力

mugging, and the miles of blank concrete wall which were perfect for graffiti!

Most of the buildings were also built to traditional British standards i. e. , jerry-built or run up on the cheap. Noises from the neighbour's flat could be heard through the flimsy walls, and the elevator was always broken. The national disenchantment with modern architects reached a peak in 1967 with the disaster at Ronan Point. Ronan Point was a twenty-two-story tower block where a gas explosion occurred. Since the construction was shoddy, one side of the building just collapsed like a pack of cards, killing three people.

Humbled architects are now a little more sensitive to the wishes of the people who will have to live in their creations. Regrettably, however, the traumatized British people remain convinced that a new building will likely be worse than what it replaces, and have developed a sense of tradition that Norman Foster describes as "fettered, cloying, nostalgic, regressive, arrested." Architects are now heavily restrained by conservation laws, and little of any interest is built.

Many celebrated British architects have done their best work abroad, where clients have more money and the public have less of a phobia toward their profession. Examples are Norman Foster's Hong Kong and Shanghai Bank Building in Hong Kong and Richard Rogers's Pompidou Centre in Paris.

Q: Why are the British so negative in their view of life?

The British are a race that is suffering from collective exhaustion. The centuries-long travails of the Industrial Revolution, of empire-building, and of two World Wars have reduced this

に満ちあふれていたこの国の人々を優柔不断な無能者の集団へと落ちぶれさせた。

新しくことを起こせる能力がアメリカ人にはあり、"やればできる"というその姿勢を讃えられているとしたら、英国人は"やってもできるわけがない"という姿勢の持ち主だと言えるだろう。なにかをするエネルギーを英国人が持ち合わせていたとしても、そのエネルギーは決してものごとを解決するためにではなく、不平をこぼすことに費やされる。不平をこぼすことが大好きな英国人の国民性は広く知られており、オーストラリアでジョークのネタになっているほどだ。

問い：「シドニー空港にジェット機が3機着陸しました。英国航空の飛行機はどれでしょう？」
答え：「エンジンを切っても、うめき続けるのが英国航空機です」

Q: 英国人はなぜあんなに個人主義的なのか？

英国人は数世紀の長きにわたり、地球上の誰にも増して強大な富と権力を手にし、もっとも成功した国家として世界に君臨した。これにより英国人は、人間が躍起になって手に入れようとする権力や物質的な繁栄といったものには、思ったほど価値がないという事実に気づくことができた。つまり人生とは偉業を成し遂げるためにあるのではなく、それぞれ自分なりにささやかに楽しむためにあるのだという知性あふれる結論に、英国という国家は何十年も前に達していたのである。

個人の利益を優先する勇気が英国人にあるのは、このためだと言われている。外国人はみずからの存在や人生を深刻に受けとめるという致命的な過ちをおかしているが、笑いの種を見つけるこ

once dynamic people to a bunch of ineffectual ditherers.

If the Americans are admired for their ability to make things happen, for their so-called *can-do* attitude, then the British have a firmly *can't-do* attitude. If they have enough energy to do anything, it is only to complain, never to set anything right. This tendency to moan is so well-recognized that it is the theme of an Australian joke.

Q: "Three jets land at Sydney airport. How do you know which one is the British Airways plane?"

A: "It doesn't stop whining even when the engine has been turned off"

Q: Why are the British so individualistic?

The British were for many centuries the world's most successful nation, with more power and more wealth than any people on earth. This enabled them to see that the things mortals strive for, such as power and material prosperity, are actually of little worth. As a nation the British therefore long ago came to the civilized conclusion that life was not for performing big, heroic deeds, but for enjoying oneself in one's own private little way.

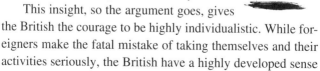

This insight, so the argument goes, gives the British the courage to be highly individualistic. While foreigners make the fatal mistake of taking themselves and their activities seriously, the British have a highly developed sense

とに秀でている英国人は、みずからを含むすべ
てのものを、皮肉と穏やかな嘲笑の入り交じった超
然とした態度で眺めることができる。このような賢
明な不真面目さを身につけたおかげで、ドイツ人
やアメリカ人、日本人らが働き過ぎで命を落とし、
国家のためというような抽象的で無意味な目標の
ためにみずからを犠牲にしているあいだ、英国人
は花壇の手入れをしたり、本を書いたり、クラシッ
クカーをいじったりというように、自分だけの楽し
みに浸る自由を手に入れたのである。

Q: 英国人はほんとうにそれほど動物が好きなのか？

狐や雉、雷鳥など、狩猟の標的にされる動物た
ちは否定するだろうが、英国人は動物好きとして
知られている。コーギー犬と馬を飼っている王室
も（その狩猟好き、釣り好きも含めて）、英国の動
物好き一家の象徴的存在だ。

英国のペットは、一般に日本のペットよりも恵ま
れた暮らしを送っている。どちらかと言えば怠惰
な英国人は、9時に出社して5時きっかりに退社す
るため、時間に余裕があり、仕事の前と後の両方
に犬を散歩に連れていくことができる。一方、日本
のペットは日本人同様、国家経済の繁栄のために
犠牲を余儀なくされており、その生活は働き過ぎ
の飼い主と同じように制限されている。1日中鎖に
つながれ、運動不足でぶくぶく太りつづけるので
ある。悪趣味なルイ・ヴィトンの"コート"に身を包
んだり、キティちゃんのリボンを飾ったり、金のか
かる犬の美容室に連れていってもらう喜びは、歩
いたり、走ったり、あたりを嗅ぎまわったりといっ
た単純で本能的な歓びを味わえないことの埋め
合わせには、とうていならないだろう。英国で日本

of the ridiculous that enables them to regard everything, themselves included, with an ironic and gently mocking detachment. This enlightened frivolity liberates them so they can contentedly cultivate gardens, write books, fiddle with vintage cars, and do whatever they please, while their German, American, or Japanese counterparts are killing themselves doing overtime, sacrificing themselves for some abstract, and ultimately hollow goal like the country's good.

Q: Do the British really love animals?

The British are famous for their love of animals, though animals like foxes, pheasants, or grouse that are hunted or shot in blood sports would probably disagree. The royal family, with their corgi dogs and their horses, (and their fondness for hunting, shooting, and fishing) are the representative British animal-loving family.

British pets generally have a better time than their Japanese counterparts. The comparatively idle British, arriving at the office at 9:00 A.M. and leaving at 5:00 P.M. prompt, have plenty of time to walk their dogs both before and after work. Japanese pets, however, just like Japanese people, are asked to make sacrifices for the greater glory of the national economy, and their lives are as restricted as their overworked owners. Chained up all day, they get fatter and fatter from lack of exercise. The pleasure of being dressed in a grotesque Louis Vuitton "coat," having a *Kitty-chan* ribbon, or being sent to an expensive doggy-hairdresser can hardly compensate for the absence of simple, natural pleasures like walking, running, and sniffing around. In Britain anyone neglecting their dogs as the Japanese do would be reported to the RSPCA (Royal Society for the Prevention of Cruelty to Animals).

人のように犬の世話を怠れば、王立動物虐待防止
協会に通報されることになるはずだ。

1993年、英国では猫の数が初めて犬を上まわっ
た。これは、英国人が仕事熱心になり、散歩に連
れていかねばならない犬のような動物にかける時
間が減った証拠であるという、輝かしい解釈がな
された。しかし少なくとも1世紀前から、一生懸命
働くことができない体質を有してきた英国人は、犬
のような無邪気で陽気な動物とさえもつき合えな
いほどに無気力になったと結論するほうが妥当と
言えそうだ。

英国ではいま、動物保護運動が高まりを見せて
いる。最近では、ヨーロッパの食通に向けた食肉
用の子牛の輸出を阻止することに情熱を傾けてい
る。動物の権利を主張する団体は、薬物検査用や
毛皮用に飼われている動物を始終檻から放して
やっている。毛皮を着てロンドン市内を歩けばペ
ンキをぶちまけられる羽目になるのが落ちだし、
毛皮店はショーウィンドウをレンガで割られる覚悟
をしなければならない。菜食主義者も激増してい
る。もっとも英国の食事のまずさを思えば、肉食
をやめたからといって高い犠牲を払ったとは言え
ないだろう。

In 1993 the British cat population overtook the British dog population for the first time. This was triumphantly interpreted as a sign that British people were working harder and therefore had less time to devote to pets, like dogs, that need exercise. The British, however, have been constitutionally incapable of hard work for at least a century, so one should probably conclude that they have become too emotionally desiccated even to get on with innocent and cheerful animals like dogs any more.

Animal rights are a popular cause in Britain now. Recently British people have got very passionate about preventing the export of veal-calves to epicurean Europeans. Animal liberation groups regularly free animals that are being bred for drug-testing or for their fur. People wearing fur coats in central London are likely to have paint thrown at them, and fur shops are likely to have a brick pitched through their window. The number of vegetarians has also risen dramatically. Of course, given the quality of British food, giving up meat can hardly be considered the supreme sacrifice.

社会

SOCIETY

Q: 英国の面積と人口は？

　"グレートブリテンおよび北部アイルランド連合王国"は、イングランド、スコットランド、ウェールズ、北アイルランド（別の島）からなる国家である。

　ヨーロッパ大陸の北西海岸沖に位置し、大陸にもっとも接近している地点におけるフランスとの距離は、わずか32キロメートルである。国土面積は24万3000平方キロメートルをわずかに下まわり（日本は37万8000平方キロメートル）、イングランドがその半分以上を占めており、スコットランド、ウェールズ、北アイルランドの順に続く。国土の一番長い地点をとると、縦に955キロメートル、横に483キロメートルだ。南部は比較的肥沃で平らであり、北部は山がちで厳しい地形となっている。

　5800万人の全人口のうち4800万人以上がイングランドに暮らし、500万人がスコットランドに、300万人がウェールズに、160万人が北アイルランドに住んでいる。イングランドの代表的な都市は、人口900万人の首都ロンドンと、人口260万人のバーミンガムである。スコットランドの首都エジンバラの人口は40万人で、工業都市グラスゴーのほぼ3分の2にすぎない。ウェールズの首都カーディフは人口27万人で、北アイルランドの首都ベルファストは30万人である。

　気候は温暖である。極端な気温の変化はないが、頻繁に雨が降り（大雨にはならないが）、太陽がまぶしいということはほとんどなく、天候は英国人が人生において耐えねばならない数々の憂鬱な事柄のなかでも最大のものとなっている。

Q: 英国の階級制度とは？

　日本人の多くは英国の階級制度を大げさに考え

Q: How big is Great Britain and how many people live there?

The United Kingdom of Great Britain and Northern Ireland, consists of England, Scotland, Wales, and Northern Ireland (which is a separate island).

The country is located off the northwest coast of the continent of Europe (to which it was once joined), and its closest point is only 32 kilometres from France. The total land area of the country is just under 243,000 square kilometres (compared to Japan's 378,000 square kilometres), with England making up more than half of this area, followed by Scotland, Wales and Northern Ireland. The country is 955 kilometres long and 483 kilometres wide at its longest and widest points. The South tends to be fertile and flat, while the North has more mountainous, harsher terrain.

Out of a total population of some 58 million, over 48 million people live in England, with 5 million Scots, 3 million Welsh and 1.6 million Northern Irish. The major cities in England are London, the capital, which has a population of 9 million, and Birmingham, with a population of 2.6 million. In Scotland Edinburgh, the capital, with a population of 400,000 is only two-thirds the size of the industrial city of Glasgow. Cardiff, the capital of Wales, has a population of 270,000, while Belfast, the capital of Northern Ireland has a population of 300,000.

The climate is mild. Although there are no extremes of temperature, it rains frequently (though feebly) and the sun seldom shines, making the weather the first of many disappointments that the British have to endure in life.

Q: What is the British class system?

Many Japanese have a very exaggerated idea of the British

すぎており、士農工商に身分が分かれていたかつ
ての封建社会の日本のような国が定めた社会階級
を想像している。海外のマスコミが英国の王室に
過剰に注目することが、英国はいまだに君主と貴
族に牛耳られている国家だという印象をいっそう
強めているようだ。

　ところが実際には、英国の階級制度は確固たる
システムとはほど遠いのである。爵位を持つ貴族
からなる上流階級も存在するものの、数の上から
見ればとるに足らないものでしかない。それでも
評論家のなかには、彼ら貴族の存在が英国人の
人生観に悪影響をおよぼしており、貴族がいるお
かげで国民は現代社会に適応した勤勉で責任感
の強い人々よりも、何世代にもわたって優雅で退
廃的な生活を送ってきた人々を尊敬するのだと指
摘する者もいる。

　日本では90パーセントの国民が、みずからを中
流階級と見なしているという統計の結果がこれま
で何度か発表されてきた。一方英国には、非常に
重要な意味を持つもう1つの区分が存在する。中
流階級は1つにまとまっているわけではなく、銀行
家や弁護士などの専門職に就く裕福な人々からな
る中の上の階級と、事務処理やデータ入力などの
低レベルの事務職に就く人々からなる中の下の階
級の2つに分かれるのである。そしてこれら2つの
グループの下に労働者階級が位置するのだ。どの
階級に属する人々も階級意識が旺盛で、自分たち
とは異なった話し方をし、違う服を着て、違った
考え方をする人々に不信の目を向ける。労働者階
級の人々は"すました"連中を信頼しようとしない
し、上流階級の人々は労働者階級の人々を"下品"
とさげすむ。誰もがみずからを、ほかの階級に相
対する存在として定義しているのである。

class system, imagining it to be a government-ordained stratification of society like the old division of Japanese society into farmers, samurai, artisans, and tradesmen. The enormous attention paid to the British royal family by the international media only serves to reinforce the impression that Britain is still a country dominated by the monarchy and the aristocracy.

The class system is, in fact, very far from systematic. While there is an upper class of titled aristocrats, they are numerically insignificant. Some commentators, however, argue that their very existence poisons the minds of the British, making them admire people who are elegantly and traditionally decadent more than people who are productive and responsible in the context of modern society.

In Japan questionnaires regularly show that 90 percent of the citizenry regard themselves as middle-class (the other 10 percent being, presumably, working class). In Britain there is one extra—and highly significant—division. The middle-class is not integrated but is split into two: the upper-middle class of highly paid professionals like bankers, lawyers, and the lower-middle class made up of lower-level office workers such as clerks, and data processors. Below these two groups there is the working class. Every group is very class-conscious, very supicious of people who speak, dress, and think unlike themselves. A working-class person will regard "posh" people with suspicion. And an upper-class person will sneer at a working-class person as being "vulgar." Everyone defines themselves by opposition to some other group.

Q: 英国ではなにが階級を決めるのか？

英国では金が階級を決めるわけではない。その証拠に億万長者のポップスターの多くも、自分たちはいまでも労働者階級の人間だと主張している。ジョン・レノンの『ワーキング・クラス・ヒーロー』という曲はその好例である。階級は広い意味では教育、つまりどんな環境で育ったかによって決まる。もっとも教育といっても、高い教育を受けたかどうかということとは無関係である。ダイアナ妃を見ても16歳で学校を出て、持っている資格と言えば調理師の免許だけなのだ。

評論家の多くが、英国の階級制度は教育制度から生まれたと指摘している。上流階級とは、基本的には私立学校に通った人々の全人口のおよそ7.5パーセントから成り立っている。私立校の多くは寄宿学校のため、きわめて学費が高く、したがって限られた人々しか入学できない。子どもたちは経済的、社会的な環境が自分とまったく同じ同級生に囲まれて育つことになる。彼らはアパルトヘイト時代の南アフリカに暮らした白人のように、一般大衆から物理的に隔離されて育つのだ。

上流階級の子弟は進学校やパブリックスクールを卒業すると一流大学へ進み、農場を経営したり軍隊に入ったりするか（チャールズ皇太子もアンドリュー王子も海軍に入隊した）、投資銀行、不動産、広告、政治などの業種に就職する。上流階級の人々は学生時代の雰囲気が保たれる職種を好む。したがって、労働者階級の人々に出会う恐れのある製造業は避けることになる。ところでこのことは、英国の製造業が劇的な不振におちいったことの、もっとも納得のいく説明と言えるだろう。異なった階級の人々が交わる唯一の職種は、法律関係の仕事である。そこでは上流階級の人々は、

Q: What determines a person's class in Britain?

It is not money that determines class status in Britain. Many pop stars who are millionaires many times over insist on emphasizing the fact that they remain working class. Think of John Lennon's song "Working-Class Hero." Class depends on education in the broadest sense, meaning how you were brought up. It has nothing to do with whether or not you are well-educated. Princess Diana, for example, left school when she was sixteen, with a single qualification in cooking!

Many commentators trace the origins of the class system to the British education sytem. The upper-class is basically all those people who go to private schools, or approximately 7.5 percent of the population. Private schools are extremely expensive because many of them are boarding schools, and consequently they are extremely exclusive. Children are brought up surrounded by other children from exactly the same socio-economic background as themselves. They are physically segregated from the mass of the population, rather like whites in apartheid South Africa!

Preparatory and public school are followed by an upper-class university, then by a career in farming or the armed forces (note that both Prince Charles and Prince Andrew served in the navy), or a career in a profession such as investment banking, property, advertising, or politics. The upper class prefer jobs in which the atmosphere of school is preserved. They therefore avoid manufacturing because there are considerable risks of encountering a person from the working class. This, by the way, is the simple most convincing explanation of the catastrophic decline of British manufacturing. About the only profession in which the classes mingle is the legal profession. Here the upper-class express their solidarity with the common people by putting them in jail!

一般大衆を刑務所にぶち込むことによって彼らとの連帯を表明している。

英国の階級制度は上流階級の人々が、悪化の一途をたどる英国経済のなかでわずかに残された割のいい仕事から、自分たち以外の人間を締めだすために作りだした機構であると主張するお堅い評論家先生も多い。これは、人は誰しも同じものを求めているという仮定に基づいた主張である。しかし、階級間の争いは一方通行ではないという事実に目を向けるべきだろう。上流階級の人々が労働者階級の人々を見下しているとするなら、労働者階級の人々もまた、上流階級の人々を蔑んでいるのである。労働者階級には独自の文化があるし、車を3台持ったり家を2軒所有したりしなくても満足できる人たちが、この世には存在するのだ。英国の階級制度に関して人々が苛立ちをおぼえるのは、上流階級の人々も労働者階級の人々も、経済的に理屈の通った行動をとらないことにあるのかもしれない。どちらの階級に属する人々も、物質的発展という考え方に心を動かされることがないようだ。英国の貴族は田舎で肥料にまみれて暮らしたがるし、労働者階級の人々は床がべたべたのパブや紙屑の散らかった馬券売場にたむろしたがる。どうして英国人はみんなMBA（経営学修士の肩書き）を取得したり、グッチやシャネルのブティックで買い物をしたりしないのだろう？ どうして彼らは物質への飽くなき欲望に衝き動かされることなく、のうのうと暮らしていられるのか？ よくもぬけぬけと満足できるものだ！ 市場経済を否定しようというのか！

こう考えてくると階級差というものは、物質主義を超越した人々に備わった、人類学上の微笑ましい特徴でしかないと言えるかもしれない。富める者と貧しき者のあいだで闘われる"階級闘争"は、

Many serious commentators present the class system in Britain as a strategic mechanism devised by the upper-class to exclude other people from the few good jobs remaining in the increasingly moribund British economy. This interpretation is based on the assumption that everyone wants the same thing. It is important, however, to recognize that the class war is a two-way battlefield, and if there is contempt from the top down, there is also contempt from the bottom up. There is a strong working-class culture, and people can be content without three cars, two houses, etc. Perhaps what annoys people about class in Britain is that neither the upper class nor the lower class are behaving in an economically rational manner. Neither group is really inspired by thoughts of material progress. British aristo-crats like to live in muck in the country. The British working class like to live in sticky-floored pubs and paper-littered bet-ting shops. Why are they not all earning MBAs, or shopping at Gucci and Chanel? How dare they not be motivated by an insatiable desire for material things! How dare they be con-tent! That is the negation of the market economy!

When you take this stand, class differences can be consid-ered as no more than a charming anthropological feature of a people that has transcended materialism. The "class war" between rich and poor is in fact no more than another game

実際のところ、世界一スポーツを愛する国家における、サッカーやクリケットやスカッシュ（あるいは政界における労働党と保守党のあいだの小競り合い）などとなんら変わるところのない一種のゲームでしかないのだ。

Q: 上流階級の人々が話す英語と普通の英語は違うのか？

"英国人が、ほかの英国人の反感を買うことなく口を開くのは不可能だ"という有名な警句からもわかるように、喋り方を聞くだけで簡単にその人の階級を知ることができる。上流階級の人々はクイーンズ・イングリッシュを話す。クイーンズ・イングリッシュ（"容認発音"とも呼ばれる）とは、地方訛りのまったくない英語である。上流階級の人々はまた、一般の人たちとは少々違った単語を用いる。たとえばトイレのことを"ルー"と言うし、長椅子のことを"ソファ"と呼ぶ。加えて、なにごとも誇張する癖が彼らにはあり、恐ろしく長い副詞や形容詞を使いたがる。"とてもおもしろい"ことは、"すばらしく魅惑的な"ことになり、"楽しい"ことは"信じられないくらい喜ばしい"ことと表現しなければならず、"とても悪いこと"は"言葉にできないほどひどい"ことと表現されるのである。

Q: パブリックスクールとはなにか？

"パブリックスクール"というのは、まことに誤解を招きやすい表現である。アメリカでパブリックスクールと言えば、文字どおり一般市民の子弟が自由に通うことのできる学校を意味する。だが英国のパブリックスクールは、きわめて排他的で学費の高い私立校である。当初は貧しい家庭の子弟に教育を授けるために設立されたことから"パブリッ

like soccer, cricket, squash (or indeed the political contest between the Labour and the Conservative parties) in the world's most sports-loving nation!

Q: Is upper-class English different from normal English?

There is a famous saying in England: "It is impossible for an Englishman to open his mouth without making some other Englishman despise him," and the easiest way to recognize someone's class is by the way he or she speaks. Upper-class people speak the Queen's English. The Queen's English (sometimes also called "received pronunciation") is English without any trace of regional accent. The upper class also uses a slightly different vocabulary from everyone else. They call a toilet a "loo," for example, and a settee a "sofa." In addition, they have a tendency to exaggerate, and so like to use very long adverbs and adjectives. Something "very interesting," becomes something "wonderfully fascinating." Something "good fun" must be "incredibly delightful," and something "very bad" will become something "unspeakably awful."

Q: What are public schools?

The name "public school" is very misleading. In America a public school is precisely what it says, a school that is free to the children of the general public. In Britain a public school is a very exclusive and expensive private school. They are called "public" because they were originally established to educate the poor, but in the nineteenth century they were hijacked by the upper middle–class and reformed in such a way as to

ク"と呼ばれているのだが、19世紀に入って中流
の上の階級に乗っとられ、金持ちしか入学できな
い学校へと造り替えられた。

ウェストミンスター、イートン、ウィンチェスター
などのように、400〜500年前に創設されたパブ
リックスクールもあるが、大半は19世紀以降に設立
された学校である。パブリックスクールの目的は、
実業家の子どもたちを貴族的に育てることにあっ
た。彼らは上流階級のものの考え方——すなわ
ち、知識（とりわけ科学的な知識）の蔑視、チーム
スポーツとチームスピリットの賛美、才能に恵まれ
たアマチュアは退屈な専門家やテクノクラートより
も価値があるという信念など——を子どもたちに
植えつけたのである。

パブリックスクールの多くは、公園や運動場に囲
まれた田舎のカントリーハウスを校舎にしている。
生徒たちは、校門によって一般世間から物理的に
隔離されており、大英帝国に日の沈むことのなか
った時代にタイムスリップしたかのような環境に暮
らしている。リンゼイ・アンダーソンという英国人
映画監督がカンヌ映画祭でグランプリを受賞した
『ifもしも……』という作品は、同性愛、体罰、寮母
との性の冒険、風変わりな教師といった、パブ
リックスクールにおける学生生活を語る上で欠かす
ことのできない古典的なモチーフをふんだんに織
り込み、1960年代のパブリックスクールの姿をユ
ーモラスに伝えている。

労働党の政治家たちは、パブリックスクールは
エリート主義に凝り固まっており、社会階級の分断
を助長していると繰り返し批判してきた。優秀な
教師が給与の高い私立校に集中する状況が続くか
ぎり、英国の教育制度を改善することは不可能だ
というのだ。労働党が政権をとるたびに、パブ
リックスクールの税制優遇措置を廃止すべきだと議

exclude anyone but the wealthy.

While some public schools such as West-minster, Eton, and Winchester were founded four or five centuries ago, the majority were only founded in the nineteenth century. They were designed to mold the children of the business classes in the aristocratic model. They taught upper-class atti-tudes—a contempt for knowledge (espe-cially scientific knowledge), a worship of team sports and team spirit, and the belief that the gifted amateur was more valuable than the dry professional or technocrat.

Many public schools are located in stately homes sur-rounded by parks and playing fields deep in the countryside. The pupils are physically separated from the ordinary people who live beyond the gates, and they consequently exist in a kind of timewarp where the sun *still* never sets on the British Empire. British film director Lindsay Andersen's prize-win-ning movie *If* paints an amusing picture of public school life in the 1960s, touching on all the classic themes—homosexuality, corporal punishment, sexual escapades with the matron, and eccentric teachers.

Public schools are frequently attacked by Labour politi-cians as socially divisive and elitist. They argue that the British education system as a whole cannot improve as long as all the best teachers choose to work in the higher-paying private schools. Every time a Labour government is elected there is much discussion of removing the public schools' tax-exempt status. Since, a large proportion of Labour politicans them-

論が戦わされる。しかし、労働党の政治家の多く
もパブリックスクール出身であることから、議論が
政策レベルにまで発展することはけっしてない。

Q: パブリックスクールの長所とは？

13歳から18歳の子どもが通うパブリックスクー
ルは、日本の中学校と高等学校に相当する。理論
上は万人に開かれているものの、入学するには大
きなハードルを2つ越えなければならない。まず
第1に、年間1万3500ポンド（約320万円）ほどかか
る学費である。第2の関門は、5年制の私立小学校
に通って試験勉強をしないかぎりとうてい合格で
きないほどむずかしい入学試験だ。

これだけの障害があるのに、なぜ親たちは子ども
をパブリックスクールに入学させたがるのだろうか？

パブリックスクールで教育を受けた子どもたち
は、統計的に見て有名大学に進学し、大学卒業後
には政治、金融、経営、医学、法律、メディアなど
の業界で成功する確率が高い。英国の"偉大で優
れた"人々（指導者的存在）の大多数はパブリック
スクール出身者だ。たとえばウィリアム王子はイー
トン校に通っているし、アンドリュー・ロイド・ウェ
ーバー（『キャッツ』や『スターライト・エクスプレス』
の作曲家）はウェストミンスター校を出ている。リ
チャード・ブランソン（ヴァージン・アトランティック
航空の創設者）はストー校出身で、トニー・ブレア
現首相はフェッツ校の出身者だ。

第2次世界大戦後、パブリックスクールは思い切
った変革を実施した。ラテン語やギリシャ語のよ
うな役に立たない教科を教えるのをやめ、生徒が
激しさを増す就職戦争に勝てるように実際的な技
術を身につけさせることに心を砕き、豊かな経済
力を背景に研究室やコンピュータ施設を建設し

selves were educated at public schools this discussion never progresses to the level of policy.

Q: What are the merits of public schools?

Public schools accept pupils between the ages of thirteen to eighteen, so they are the equivalent of junior high and high schools in Japan . Theoretically open to all, there are two significant barriers to entry to public school. First, the fees are about £13,500 per year (about ¥3.2 million). Second, it is very difficult to pass the exams to get into a public school without already having had several years preparation at a special fee-paying preparatory school.

Given these barriers to entry, why should parents want to send their children to such schools?

People who have received a public school education are statistically more likely to get into better universities and then go on to have successful careers in politics, finance, industrial management, medicine, the law, and the media. Even now the overwhelming proportion of "the great and the good" (the leaders of public life) in Britain were educated at public schools. To give some examples: Prince William is at Eton, Andrew Lloyd-Webber (composer of *Cats* and *Starlight Express*) went to Westminster, Richard Branson (founder of Virgin Atlantic Airways) went to Stowe, and Tony Blair, the current prime minister, went to Fettes.

Since World War II public schools have modernized dramatically. They no longer teach only impractical subjects like Latin and Greek, but have used their considerable financial power to build laboratories and computer facilities so that their students can develop practical skills for an ever more competitive job market. Many have started to admit female students,

た。女子学生を受け入れた学校も多く、外国人学生も増えている。階級主義的ではあるにしても、パブリックスクールが提供する教育の質の高さは疑問の余地がないところだ。公的試験におけるパブリックスクールの実績には驚くべきものがある。ロンドンのウェストミンスター校は、なんと百パーセントの合格率を誇っている。

Q: 英国人は一般にどんな宗教を信じているのか？

英国では数々の宗教のなかで、2600万人の教会員を有する英国国教会（イギリス国教会とも呼ばれる）が最大の信者数を誇っている。第2位が570万人の教会員を有するカトリック教会で、その他の"非国教会系教会"の教会員が合計で630万人にのぼっており、全体では3800万人を上まわる国民がキリスト教徒ということになる。

上記の各教会は基本的な教義は同じだが、組織には若干の違いがある。英国国教会の首長は国王だが、ローマカトリック教会を率いるのは教皇である。非国教会系教会は基本的に、英国国教会の位階性を拒否したプロテスタント教会だ。

女王を首長とする英国国教会は、豊かな中産階級が豊かな中産階級のために運営する組織であることから、"礼拝する保守党"と揶揄されることが多い。とはいえ、国内でもっとも古く、建築物としても価値ある教会を所有しているのは英国国教会であり、ダイアナ妃の結婚式や葬儀を観た人ならわかるとおり、英国国教会は盛大なショーを興行する能力を備えている。もっとも、だからといって英国人が信心深いということにはならない。英

while the number of foreign students is also growing. However socially divisive public schools may be, the quality of education they provide is not in doubt. The success of the public schools in public examinations is nothing short of remarkable. Westminster School in London, for example, has a pass rate of 100 percent!

Q: What religion do the majority of British people follow?

In Britain the Anglican Church (also called the Church of England) has over 26 million members and has the greatest number of followers. The Catholic church is second, with 5.7 million members, while other "non-conformist" churches have a further 6.3 million members between them, bringing the Christian total to just over 38 million.

While all the above churches share the same fundamental beliefs, they are organized somewhat differently. The Church of England is headed by the monarch, while the Roman Catholic church is led by the pope. The non-conformist churches are basically Protestant churches that refuse to accept the hierarchy of the Church of England.

The Church of England, of which the queen is the head, is frequently mocked as "the Conservative Party at prayer", meaning that it is an organization run by the prosperous middle classes for the prosperous middle classes. Certainly, the Church of England has all the oldest and most architecturally distinguished churches and—as anyone who watched Princess Diana's wedding or funeral knows—they can put on a splendid pageant. Whether anyone has any faith or not is quite a different matter. The English, at least, are cold and unimaginative,

国人は冷淡で想像力に欠ける国民であり、気質的
に宗教に不向きである。

いまや多民族国家となった英国では、キリスト
教以外の宗教を信仰する人が増え、その数は300
万人近くに達しており、なかでも最大のグループは
信徒数120万を誇るイスラム教である。モスクの尖
塔や、イスラム教徒がブラッドフォード（イングラン
ド北部の都市）でサルマン・ルシュディの『悪魔の
詩』を燃やしたときのようなときおり発生する焚書
の炎によって、英国の都市は近頃活気づいている。

1996年に行われた政府調査によると、英国人の
95パーセントがなんらかの宗教を信じているとい
う。そのうち11パーセントは定期的に宗教儀式に
出席しているが、どんな形の宗教儀式にも出席し
たことのない人が過半数を占め、残りの人々は1
年に1、2度——クリスマスか結婚式や葬式に出席
することがあるだけだと答えた。ここが、かなり
多くの人たちが日曜日ごとに教会へ通うアメリカと
大きく異なる点であり、だからこそアメリカ人はふ
しだらな大統領にお灸をすえたり、サダム・フセイ
ンのような浅黒い異教徒に対して十字軍（と巡航
ミサイル）を派遣したりする“骨太の”キリスト教徒
になることができるのである。

＊数字は英国統計局発行の『社会動向28』より

Q: 現在の英国の人種構成は？

英国の全人口のおよそ6パーセントは少数民族
で、そのなかでも比較的大きなグループは、イン
ド人（90万人）、パキスタン人とバングラデシュ人
（80万人）、西インド諸島出身の黒人（50万人）、ア
フリカ系黒人（30万人）である。

英国が現在のような多民族国家になったのは、
1950年代末から1960年代初頭にかけて起きた大

temperamentally unsuited to religion.

Since Britain is now a multiracial society, the number of people belonging to non-Christian religions has grown dramatically to a total of just under 3 million, with the 1.2 million Muslims the largest group in this category. The cityscape of British cities has recently been enlivened by the minarets of mosques and the occasional bookburning, as when the Muslims in Bradford publicly burnt Salman Rushdie's *Satanic Verses*.

In responding to a 1996 government survey 95 percent of British people said they had some sort of religious belief. Of these 11 percent attended religious services regularly. The majority of people never attended any form of service, while the rest said they might go once or twice a year—at Christmas or for weddings and funerals. This is a key difference with the United States where a far higher proportion of people go to church every Sunday, enabling Americans to be the "muscular" Christians they are, punishing lewd presidents and launching crusades (and cruise missiles) against swarthy infidels like Saddam Hussein.

＊All figures come from Social Trends 28/Office for National Statistics

Q: What is the ethnic make-up of modern Britain?

Ethnic minorities make up around 6 percent of Britain's total population, with Indians (0.9 million), Pakistanis and Bangladeshis (0.8 million), Black Caribbeans (0.5 million) and Black Africans (0.3 million) making up the most significant groups.

Contemporary Britain's multicultural society has its origins in the waves of immigration that took place in the late

規模な移民流入がきっかけだった。ほんの短いあいだだけヨーロッパのほかの国々より景気がよかった英国は労働力不足に直面し、英連邦（旧植民地）から移民を受け入れることによって労働力を補おうとした。移民たちは、ロンドンやイングランド中部および北部の大都市を中心に住みつき、特殊技能を必要としない低賃金の仕事に就いた。

1957年、当時の首相は英国の繁栄を誇り、英国の未来は"かつて経験したことのないほどすばらしい"ものになるだろうと有権者に請け合った。だが残念なことに英国は、そのころのようなすばらしい状況を二度と経験することができなかった。1960年代に入ると、英国経済はライバルに追い抜かれはじめた。1970年代半ば以降は、失業者が街にあふれる状況が当たり前になり、少数民族は国家平均を大きく上まわる失業率に苦しむことになった。白人の失業率は14パーセントだが、黒人の若者の失業率は35パーセント、パキスタン人とバングラデシュ人は31パーセント、インド人は26パーセントである。

それでも、経済的にはお先真っ暗というわけではない。少数民族は働き者なのである。その証拠にメインストリートにはかならず中華料理店とインド料理店が店を出しているし、数え切れないほどのインド人がコンビニエンスストアを経営している。学位を取得するインド人の割合は白人と同じくらい高く、頭脳労働に就くインド人が激増している。娯楽産業においても、歌手のシャーデー（ナイジェリア人とイギリス人を両親に持つ）やシール（ナイジェリア人、ブラジル人、西インド諸島出身の黒人の血を引く）、短距離走者のリンフォード・クリスティやボクサーのプリンス・ナジーム・ハメドなどの有名スポーツ選手らが、大金を稼いでいる。

それでも、少数民族は日常生活における数々の

1950s and early 1960s. Britain's booming economy—for a very brief time healthier than those of its European counterparts—was hampered by a labour shortage, which immigration from the Commonwealth (former colonies) was designed to solve. The newcomers tended to settle in London and the centers of the big cities in the Midlands and the North, where they took chiefly unskilled, low-paid work.

In 1957 the prime minister, boasting of Britain's prosperity, famously told the electorate that they'd "never had it so good." Unfortunately, they were never to have it so good again. Enter the 1960s, and the British economy was quite plainly losing ground to its rivals. Since the mid-1970s, mass unemployment has become the norm, and the ethnic minorities suffer from unemployment rates well in excess of the national average. Over 35 percent of young blacks, 31 percent of Pakistanis and Bangladeshis, and 26 percent of Indians are without a job, while the average for whites is 14 percent.

The economic picture, however, is not all gloom and doom. Ethnic minorities work hard. Obvious testimony to this are the Chinese and Indian restaurants on every main street, and the numerous Indian-operated convenience stores. Indians are now as likely to have a degree as whites, and are making dramatic advances in white-collar business. In entertainment, singers like Sade (of mixed Nigerian/English parentage) and Seal (Nigerian, Brazilian, Afro-Caribbean) and sports celebrities like the sprinter Linford Christie and the boxer Prince Nassem Hamed are minting money.

Nonetheless, ethnic minorities, in addition to having to

困難と戦わねばならない上に、差別や暴力の危険
にもさらされている。少数民族は、暴力の標的に
される不安を白人の2倍も強く感じているという。
国民戦線や英国国民党のような暴力的な政党——
クー・クラックス・クランのヨーロッパ版——も、扇
情的な演説やデモを律儀に実行している。

　治安当局が障害となることもある。1981年にロ
ンドンとリバプールで起きた暴動は、警察による
少数民族へのいやがらせが引き金だったと言わ
れている。

　移住先として英国を見る場合、仕事はないにし
ても、少なくとも戦争や洪水や飢饉もない場所と
いうのが最大の褒め言葉かもしれない。

＊数字は英国統計局発行の『社会動向28』より

Q: "サー"という称号にはどんな重みがあるのか？

　毎年元旦と女王の公式の誕生日になると、女王
が発表した叙勲リストが新聞に掲載される。誰に
叙勲を授けるのかを決めるのは、実際には女王で
はなく政治家である（政権党に多額の献金をした
裕福な実業家がナイトの身分や貴族の地位を手に
入れることが多い）。毎年数千人にのぼる人々が、
国家への貢献を評価されて爵位を授けられてい
る。

　爵位には3つの種類がある。
　まず最初は貴族の位である。すなわち、公爵、
伯爵、子爵、男爵の位を授けられ、上院に出席す
る——あるいは居眠りする——権利を与えられる
のである。最近貴族になった（正式には"叙せら
れた"と表現する）人といえば、男爵の位を得たサ

contend with tremendous practical difficuties, also face discrimination and violence. They are more than twice as afraid of being the victim of violent crime than whites. And brutish political parties like the National Front and the British National Party—a kind of European Ku Klux Klan—make it their business to make provocative speeches and demonstrations.

Problems can also be caused by the side of law and order. Police harassment is said to have started the 1981 riots in London and Liverpool.

As a place to emigrate to perhaps the best that can be said of Great Britain now is that though there may be no jobs, there is, at least, no war, no flood, and no famine.

*Figures from Social Trends 28/Office for National Statistics

Q: What is the significance of the title "Sir"?

Every year, on the first day of the New Year and on her official birthday, the queen publishes an honors list which is printed in the newspapers. In fact the selection of people who are honored is not made by the queen herself, but by politicians. (Rich businessmen who have made large donations to the party in power tend to receive knighthoods and peerages). Several thousand people each year receive honors for services to their country.

There are three kinds of honors.

First, you can be made a peer. This means you become a duke, an earl, a viscount, or a baron and have the right to sit— even to snooze—in the House of Lords. Recent examples of people who have been made peers (or "elevated to the peerage" as the expression goes) are Mrs. Thatcher, the former

ッチャー元首相や、作家のジェフリー・アーチャーを挙げることができる。貴族は男性の場合は"卿"、女性の場合は"レディ"という称号で呼ばれる。貴族になれる人の数はきわめて限られている。

次に、勲章や褒章の類がある。ガーター勲位やバース勲位のような、授与数が定められており、ごく少数の人々のみに与えられる歴史ある勲位から、大英帝国勲位のような"スーパーマーケット勲章"まで多種多様である。ビートルズは英国に外貨をもたらした功績により、1965年にMBE勲章（大英帝国勲位のメンバー）を与えられた。

最後がナイトの位だ。ナイトの位をもらうと、男性は"サー"の称号で、その妻は"レディ"の称号で呼ばれる。女性がナイトの位を得た場合は、"デイム"の称号で呼ばれる。ナイトの大半は、定年を目前にした国家公務員をはじめとする退屈で徳の高い人々だが、『スター・ウォーズ』でオビ・ワン・ケノービを演じたアレック・ギネスやビートルズのポール・マッカートニーのような芸能界の有名人や、小型車ミニを設計したアレック・イシゴーニスもナイトの位を授与された。

Q: 英国の教育制度はどんな仕組みになっているのか？

英国の義務教育は、5歳で通いはじめる小学校から始まる。11歳で中学校に入学し、中学校で2種類の国家試験を受ける。これらの試験は、中等教育終了一般試験（16歳で受験）と、教育終了一般試験Aレベル（18歳で受験）と呼ばれている。ほとんどどんな職業に就く場合でも、中等教育終了一般試験に合格していることが最低必要条件となっており、学生は一般に英語と数学を含めて6課目から7課目の教科を受験する。大学への進学を希望する学生は、さらにAレベル試験を受験する。

prime minister, now Baroness Thatcher, and Jeffrey Archer, the novelist. Peers are adressed as "Lord" or "Lady." The number of peers created is extremely limited.

Second, you can receive some kind of medal or decoration. Orders range from ancient and highly exclusive ones with a limit of the number of living recipients, such as the Order of the Garter and the Order of the Bath, to "supermarket orders" like the Order of the British Empire. The Beatles in 1965 were awarded MBEs (Member of the Order of the British Empire) for their contribution to British export.

Finally, there are knighthoods. Receiving a knighthood means that you are addressed as "Sir" and your wife as "Lady." If a woman is knighted she is addressed as "Dame." While most knights are dull and worthy people like civil servants approaching retirement age, flashy characters from showbusiness like Alec Guinness, who played Obi Wan Kinobi in *Star Wars*, Paul McCartney of the Beatles, and Alec Issigonis, the designer of the mini, get knighted, too.

Q: How is the British education system organized?

Compulsory education in Britain starts with elementary school at the relatively late age of five. At the age of eleven children move on to secondary school, where they take two sets of national examinations. These are GCSEs (taken at the age of sixteen) and GCE A Levels (taken at the age of eighteen). Most children take six or seven GCSEs, including English Language and Maths, which are the minimum qualifications needed for most sorts of job, while three or four A Levels are taken by pupils who intend to continue their education at university. Usually students select a group of science subjects (e.g.,

Aレベルにおいては通常、理数系（数学、物理学、化学など）の課目か文系（フランス語、英語、歴史など）の課目のどちらかを選択する。Aレベル試験の成績いかんによって、どの大学に入学できるかが決まることになる。現在では、中等教育を終了した学生の3人に1人が大学に進学している。

かつては子どもたちは11歳になると試験を受け、成績の優秀な生徒はグラマースクールへ、あまり成績のよくない生徒はセカンダリー・モダンスクールへ進学するという制度が採用されていた。しかしこれは"階級制度"を温存する恐れがあったことから、労働党政府は居住地域のみによって学校を決めるコンプリヘンシブスクール（総合制中等学校）制度を1964年に導入した。無差別に子どもを受け入れるこのような制度につきものの質の低下を避けるために、グラマースクールの多くが授業料の必要な私立校に生まれ変わり、子どもを私立校に通わせる親が増加した。

国際試験の結果を見ると、英国の子どもたちの学力は、数学においてはフランス、カナダ、ドイツ各国の子どもたちよりも下だったが、アメリカやスペインよりは上で、科学はきわめて優秀だった。

知識がものを言う世界経済においては、優れた教育制度が国家経済の安定に欠かせない要素だと誰もが感じている。このため政治家たちは、教育にもっとも力を入れていると力説したがる。その結果、かつては失業者数の算出にしか使われることのなかった巧妙な数字操作が、最近では教育に関する統計にも活かされるようになった。大学進学者数は飛躍的に伸びた……なぜなら、工芸専門学校が大学に昇格して、大学数が2倍に増えたからである。中等教育終了一般試験の合格率も上昇した……なぜなら、試験が簡単になったからだ。

美辞麗句とは裏腹に、公立校の大半は資金不足

Maths, Physics, Chemistry) or arts subjects (e.g.; French, English, History) for their A Levels. The quality of A level results attained determines which university a student can get into. One out of three students now goes to university.

The old education system, which administered tests at the age of eleven, divided children according to ability, sending the brighter ones to grammar school and the less academically able ones to secondary modern schools. Since this was regarded as likely to perpetuate the "class system," in 1964 the Labour government introduced comprehensive schools, which selected children on no criteria other than where they lived. To avoid the slide in standards inherent in such an undiscriminating approach, many grammar schools became private and fee-paying, while the number of parents sending their children to private schools increased.

In international tests British children finished below their French, Canadian, and German counterparts but above the U.S. and Spain for maths, while showing remarkable strength in science.

In a knowledge-based global economy, a good education system is accepted as a crucial precondition for the economic health of the nation. Politicians therefore like to claim that education is one of their top priorities. As a result, education statistics have become subject to the same kind of crafty massage that used to be reserved for unemployment figures. More students are going to university. . . because the number of universities was doubled by upgrading all polytechnic colleges into universities! GCSE pass rates have improved. . . because the exams are made easier!

Despite the platitudes, state schools are generally under-

と多すぎる生徒数に悩まされている。教師の給与
はヨーロッパ平均に比べて低く、そのために労働
意欲の低下を招いている。

最後に、英国では地域によって教育に対する姿
勢が違うことに目を向ける必要があるだろう。スコ
ットランド人はきわめて教育熱心だが、イギリス人
は教育にあまり関心がない。

Q: オックスフォード大学とケンブリッジ大学はなぜ名門校なのか?

英国にはさまざまなタイプの大学がある。グラ
スゴーやエディンバラなどのスコットランドの大学、
19世紀に産業都市に設立されたいわゆる赤レン
ガ大学(1828年に創設されたロンドン大学もその
1つ)や、1960年代に生まれたサセックスやイース
ト・アングリアをはじめとする戦後に創設された
大学、そして1990年代初頭に大学扱いになるまで
は工芸専門学校と呼ばれていた新設大学などで
ある。

オックスフォードとケンブリッジは、他の大学と
比べものにならないほど古い歴史を持つ大学だ。
ケンブリッジが創設されたのは800年も前のこと
で、オックスフォードの歴史はそれよりさらに遡る。
19世紀に入るまでは、イングランドで大学と言え
ばこの2校しかなかったために、歴史上の重要人
物の大半がどちらかの大学で学んだ。このような
才能の独占はいくらか緩和されたものの、今日に
いたるまで続いている。

オックスフォードとケンブリッジは良好なライバ
ル関係にある。どちらも規模はほぼ同じで、およ
そ1万5000人の学生が30前後の独立した学寮で学
んでいる。両校は毎年ボートレースやラグビーの
対校試合を開催している。オックスフォード大学の

funded and overcrowded. Teachers are badly paid, by European standards, and are consequently demoralized.

Finally, it is important to note that attitudes to education vary around Britain. The Scots take their schools very seriously, the English much less so.

Q: Why are Oxford and Cambridge so prestigious?

The British education system contains many different types of university. There are the Scottish universities such as Glasgow and Edinburgh, the so-called redbrick universities established in the big industrial towns in the nineteenth century (including London University that dates from 1828), the postwar universities such as Sussex and East-Anglia dating from the 1960s, and finally the "new universities" which were called polytechnics until their status was changed in the early 1990s.

Oxford and Cambridge are by far the most ancient universities in England. Cambridge was founded 800 years ago, and Oxford is even older. Until the nineteenth century they were the only universities in England, meaning that nearly everyone of importance had attended one or the other institution. This monopoly of talent continues today, though in a somewhat watered-down form.

There is a friendly rivalry between them. They are both about the same size with about 15,000 students divided among thirty or so independent colleges. They compete with each other in the annual Oxford-Cambridge boat race, and the Varsity rugby match. Oxonians refer mockingly to Cambridge as

学生はケンブリッジを"もう1つの場所"と呼び、ケンブリッジの学生もまたオックスフォードを同じ表現で呼んでいる。

ただし、両校の校風は大きく異なっている。ケンブリッジの学生は一般に、真面目で内向的で科学の分野に秀でた若者たちだというイメージを持たれている。卒業生のなかには、アイザック・ニュートン卿、チャールズ・ダーウィン、ジョン・メイナード・ケインズ、スティーヴン・ホーキングらがいる。

一方のオックスフォードは、ケンブリッジよりも世俗的な雰囲気を持つ大学で、政治家や芸術家として名をあげる日を夢見る軽薄で派手好みの社交的な学生であふれかえっている。オックスフォードのなかの1学寮にすぎないクライストチャーチ学寮だけでも13人もの首相を輩出しており、彼らの名をインターネットのホームページに誇らしげに掲げている。近年オックスフォードを卒業した政治家を見ても、ビル・クリントン、トニー・ブレア、男爵の爵位を持つサッチャー元首相ら錚々たる顔ぶれだ。芸術の分野では、ジョナサン・スウィフト(『ガリバー旅行記』)、ルイス・キャロル(『不思議の国のアリス』)、グレアム・グリーン(『第三の男』)、ウィリアム・モリスやエドワード・バーンジョーンズなどのラファエル前派の画家、"ミスター・ビーン"のローワン・アトキンソンらを世に送りだしてきた。

英国では数百年の長きにわたり、大学教育を受けることができるのはひと握りの裕福な人々に限られていた。このためオックスフォードとケンブリッジは、パント舟に乗ってシャンペンをあおり、贅沢なサマーパーティで一晩じゅう踊り騒ぐ退廃的な貴族たちの学校にすぎないと見る人は多い。しかし、両校とももずかしい入学試験を課し、能力ある者に平等に開かれた大学であろうと努めている。とはいえ、両校の威信はいまも健在である。

"the other place," while Cantabrians refer to Oxford in the same way.

There are, nonetheless, important differences in tone between them. Cambridge people are thought of as serious, introverted, and exceling in the sciences. Graduates include Sir Isaac Newton, Charles Darwin, John Maynard Keynes and Stephen Hawking.

Oxford, on the other hand, is a much more worldly place full of superficial, flamboyant extroverts eager to make a name for themselves in politics or the arts. Christchurch, a single college at Oxford, proudly lists 13 Old Boy prime ministers on its web-site! Recent political graduates of the university include Bill Clinton, Tony Blair, and Baroness Thatcher. In the arts Oxford has produced Jonathan Swift (*Gulliver's Travels*), Lewis Carroll (*Alice's Adventures in Wonderland*), Graham Greene (*The Third Man*), the Pre-Raphaelite painters William Morris and Edward Burne-Jones, and Rowan Atkinson "Mr. Bean".

For many centuries university education was limited to the moneyed few. As a result many people associate Oxford and Cambridge with decadent aristocrats quaffing champagne in punts and dancing all night at lavish summer balls. Both universities, however, strive to be egalitarian and meritocratic with entrance by competitive exam. Nonetheless, their social cachet remains intact. Prince Charles and Prince Edward went to Cambridge, while Crown Prince Naruhito and Princess Masako both went to Oxford.

　チャールズ皇太子もエドワード王子もケンブリッジで学んだし、皇太子徳仁殿下と皇太子妃雅子殿下は、どちらもオックスフォードに留学した。

　オックスフォードとケンブリッジは、いまなお発展しつづけている。オックスフォード大学には最近日産日本問題研究所ができたし、ケンブリッジにもつい先頃経営学研究所を開設した。

Oxford and Cambridge continue to develop. Oxford, for example, has recently added the Nissan Institute of Japanese Studies, while Cambridge has just opened a new Instititute of Management Studies.

文化

ENTERTAINMENT

Q: 英国生まれの有名ポップ・グループは？

現代のロックンロールは、1950年代にアメリカの
バディ・ホリーやエルヴィス・プレスリーらソロシン
ガーや、ビル・ヘイリーとコメッツのようなバンド
から生まれた。しかし1960年代初頭から半ばにか
けては、英国のグループが世界を席巻した。最初
にスーパースターの座にのしあがった英国のグル
ープは、1965年に"サティスファクション"で全世界
にその名を轟かせたローリング・ストーンズとビー
トルズ（1964年のアメリカのビルボード・ホット100
で上位5曲を独占）である。当時アメリカのマスコ
ミが"英国の侵略"と評したほど、英国出身グルー
プの人気は高かった。

それ以後も、英国は数々の人気ミュージシャン
を生みだしてきた。英国のバンドは独創性に富み
実験的だという点で注目に値する。ピンク・フロイ
ドとクリームはサイケデリック・ロックの先駆けとな
ったし、レッド・ツェッペリンはヘビー・メタルの祖
としていまでも崇められている。デビッド・ボウイ、
ロキシー・ミュージック、クィーンは、グラム・ロッ
クという分野を創りあげた。そして、セックス・ピ
ストルズは最初のパンクロッカーだった。

Q: 英国の音楽とアメリカの音楽の違いは？

アメリカの音楽は英国の音楽に比べて保守的で
ある。広大な国土を有するアメリカでは、ヒットチ
ャートをのぼるにもそれだけ時間がかかるのだ。
しかもアメリカ人は、さわやかで明るい音楽以外
は、破壊的で不健全だと見なす傾向にある。アメ
リカ人が音楽を聞くとき、その評価の基準になる
のは、ドライブしながら聴くのにふさわしいかとい

Q: What famous pop groups have emerged from the U.K.?

Modern rock and roll music originated in the United States in the 1950s with solo performers such as Buddy Holly and Elvis Presley, and bands like Bill Haley and the Comets. From the early to middle 1960s, however, British acts achieved enormous international success. The first British groups to attain superstar status were The Beatles (who held all the top five positions in the American Billboard Hot 100 in 1964) and the Rolling Stones, who became internationally famous in 1965 with "I Can't Get No Satisfaction." Such was the success of British bands that the American press spoke of a "British invasion."

Britain has continued to produce highly successful performers ever since. It is important to be aware of the originality and innovativeness of British bands. Pink Floyd and Cream pioneered psychedelic rock; Led Zeppelin are revered as the fathers of heavy metal; David Bowie, Roxy Music, and Queen were the leading proponents of glam rock; and the Sex Pistols were the original punk rockers.

Q: What's the difference between British and American music?

In comparison to British music, American music tends to be very conservative. The United States is vast, and it takes any record a proportionately long time to get the necessary airplay to make it up the charts. Americans are also conditioned to regard anything that is not bland and cheerful as subversive and unwholesome. The criteria by which American's judge music is; Is it good for driving my car to? America is the mecca

うことなのだ。資本主義のメッカであるアメリカで
は、音楽でさえ"耳で聴くハンバーガー"とでも呼
ぶべき商品の1つになっている。

これに比べて、英国の音楽はきわめて実験的で
ある。国家そのものも音楽市場も比較的小さいた
めに、ヒット曲はわずか数週間のうちにチャートを
せわしなく上下し、さまざまな音楽が現れては姿
を消していく。英国では音楽は、アメリカのような
エネルギッシュで力強く、愛国心に富んだもので
ある必要はない（猥褻な歌詞で批判されることの
多いラップでさえ、撃ちあったり強姦したりするだ
けの気概を持つ人々の音楽だ）。パンクが表現し
たのは社会からの疎外感だったし、ポストパンク
は暗い気分と失業を歌ったものばかりだった。テ
クノやジャングルにいたっては、麻薬でもやらない
かぎり楽しむことは不可能である。英国の音楽
は、社会の暗部を心ゆくまで探求する権利を手に
していると言えるだろう。

レコードを買う音楽ファンもまた、商業的に成功
したグループを忌み嫌う。成功したミュージシャ
ンは"魂を売り渡して""金のためだけに"音楽を
やっていると批判されるのだ。こうした考えに凝
り固まった英国人は、主流以外の新しいグループ
を見つけだしては賞賛しようとする。NME（ニュ
ー・ミュージカル・エキスプレス）のような音楽誌や
ジョン・ピールに代表されるディスク・ジョッキー
も、アヴァンギャルドなミュージシャンを探したが
る英国人の性癖を助長している。目新しいものを
どこまでも追い求めようとする姿勢の裏には、古
いものはなにもかも悪いという乱暴な論理が横た
わっている。ジョン・レノンが凶弾に倒れた時に英
国人が冷淡な反応しか見せなかったのもこのため
である。あの時、ヒッピーの守護神を失ったアメリ
カ大衆はヒステリックに騒ぎたてたが、英国人に

of capitalism, so its music tends automatically to be commercial, a kind of "aural hamburger."

The British music scene is highly experimental. The country itself and the music market are relatively small, enabling songs to scuttle up and down the charts in a matter of a few weeks, making for a high turnover of music. Unlike in the United States, British music is under no idealistic obligation to be patriotic by being energetic, dynamic, and positive. (Even rap, which is often attacked for its obscene lyrics, is about people with enough get-up-and-go to shoot or rape one another.) Punk expressed social alienation, Post Punk was all about gloom and unemployment, and techno and jungle are musical styles that cannot be enjoyed without drugs. British music has a license to explore the dark side of society as much as it wants.

Much of the British record-buying public also have a principle of disliking commercially successful groups. They are said to have "sold out" and to be making music "only for the money."  This way of thinking forces British people to look outside the mainstream to find new groups to admire. This practice of seeking out the avant-garde is encouraged by music papers such as the NME (New Musical Express) and disc jockeys such as John Peel. The flipside of this perpetual demand for novelty is the harsh philosophy that anything old is bad. Hence the coolness of the British response to the shooting of John Lennon. The American public reacted with mass hysteria—they had been robbed of the patron saint of hippiedom—but for the British, John Lennon was already a has-

とってジョン・レノンはすでに過去の人であり、音楽の進化という鎖のなかの1つの輪（重要な輪ではあるにしても）でしかなかった。数十年間にわたってミュージックシーンに君臨しつづける英雄など、英国には存在しないのである。

Q: 英国のおもな新聞は？

英国の新聞は、英国の社会階層をそのまま反映している。したがって、日刊紙はおおまかに3つのグループに分けることができる。その頂点にあるのは、右寄りの『デイリー・テレグラフ』、左寄りの『ガーディアン』、経済記事中心の『フィナンシャル・タイムズ』などのいわゆる高級紙で、次に来るのが『デイリー・メイル』をはじめとする中間層をターゲットにしたプチブル紙である。数あるなかで最下層に位置するのが、右寄りの『サン』や労働党支持の『ミラー』などに代表される大衆紙、あるいは"どぶ"新聞だ。高級紙は普通サイズの新聞で、中間紙や大衆紙はタブロイド版である。

発行部数を見ると、大衆紙はその名のとおり大衆的で、主な大衆紙（『サン』、『ミラー』、『デイリー・スター』）の発行部数の合計は1日あたり700万部を超えている。中間紙2紙（『デイリー・メイル』、『デイリー・エクスプレス』）の販売部数も合計すれば350万部を超えるが、高級紙（『デイリー・テレグラフ』『タイムズ』『ガーディアン』『フィナンシャル・タイムズ』『インディペンデント』）各紙の販売部数は合計しても300万に満たない。つまり、英国の高級紙の販売部数は日本とは対照的に、日刊紙全体の3分の1以下にすぎないのである。

高級紙は国内外の事件を網羅しており、報道記事においても社説においても、できるかぎり客観的な姿勢を保とうとする。

been, just one link (albeit an important one) in the chain of musical evolution. The British music-buying public has no long-term heroes.

Q: What are the main British newspapers?

British newspapers reflect the stratification of British society. The daily papers thus divide into three broad groups. At the top there are the so-called quality papers like the right-wing *Daily Telegraph*, the left-wing *Guardian*, and the business-oriented *Financial Times*. Next come *petit bourgeois* mid-market papers like the *Daily Mail*. Finally, at the bottom of the heap, is the popular or "gutter" press represented by the right-leaning *Sun* and the Labour supporting *The Mirror*. The quality papers are broadsheets, while the mid-market and popular papers are tabloids.

In terms of circulation, the popular press lives up to its name, with the three main papers (*Sun*, *Mirror*, *Daily Star*) selling a total of about 7 million copies per day. The two mid-market papers (*Daily Mail*, *Daily Express*) achieve total sales of over 3.5, while the qualities (*Daily Telegraph*, *The Times*, *Guardian*, *Financial Times*, *Independent*) achieve total sales of less than 3 million copies. British quality papers, then, in sharp contrast to Japan, account for less than one-third of total sales of daily newspapers.

The quality papers attempt to give comprehensive coverage of domestic and foreign events, and try to achieve some degree of objectivity both in their reporting and their editorials.

　これに対して中間紙は、紙面が小さいという単純な理由のために記事の分量が少なくなっている。内容のほうは、世界を善玉と悪玉が戦うお伽芝居に見たてて、より大衆受けする論調を採用しがちである。頻繁に登場する悪玉は、労働者階級に属する労働組合の指導者だ。中間紙はまた、王室や有名人に関する"事情通"のゴシップをさかんに掲載することによって、社会階層を這いのぼりたいと願う読者の嗜好に対応している。

　大衆紙はあらゆる報道を紙面から排除すること（血なまぐさい殺人事件や悲惨な災害のニュースは例外として）にほぼ成功しており、その代わりにセックス・スキャンダル、ミュージシャンやテレビタレントのゴシップ、信じられないような本当の話、微に入り細をうがったスポーツ記事、トップレス女性の写真などの掲載に力を入れている（女性のトップレス写真は英国フェミニストの不興を買っている。ポルノ小説やポルノビデオの紹介記事、ピンクサロンのきわめて写実的な広告などがふんだんに掲載された日本のタブロイド紙を見たら、英国のフェミニストはどんな反応を示すだろうか？）。

＊『British Civilization: An Introduction』（ルートリッジ社刊）の統計より

Q: ルパート・マードックは英国のメディアをどう変えたか？

　英国の新聞のかなりの部分はオーストラリアの世界的なメディア王、ルパート・マードックに牛耳られている。『サン』も『タイムズ』（日刊紙）も『ニューズ・オブ・ザ・ワールド』も『サンデー・タイムズ』（日曜紙）も、すべてルパート・マードックが率いるニューズ・インターナショナルというコングロマリットの傘下にある。

　英国におけるマードックの経営方針はオーストラリアの場合と同じく、大衆に迎合して売り上げ

The mid-market papers contain less news for the simple reason that they are physically smaller. They often have a more crowd-pleasing tone, interpreting the world as a pantomine stage where "goodies" and "baddies" fight it out. Working-class trades-union leaders are popular villains. Mid-market papers cater to the upward social aspirations of their readership by featuring a great deal of "in-the-know" gossip about the Royal Family and other celebrities.

The popular press manages more or less to exclude all news (with the exception of grisly murders or horrible disasters), preferring instead to concentrate on sex scandals, gossip about pop stars and TV personalities, amazing-but-true stories, extensive sports reporting, and pictures of topless girls. (These last cause much anxiety among British feminists. One can only wonder what their reaction would be to the Japanese tabloid press with its erotic novels, video reviews, and highly descriptive advertisements for Pink Salons!)

*Statistics from British Civilization: An Introduction (Routledge)

Q: How has Rupert Murdoch changed the British media?

Rupert Murdoch, an Australian press baron, controls a large proportion of the British press. *The Sun* and *The Times* (dailies), and *The News of the World* and the *Sunday Times* (Sunday papers) are all part of his News International conglomerate.

Murdoch's policy in Britain, as in Australia, has been to increase sales by going

を伸ばすことである。『サン』にトップレス女性の写真を初めて掲載したのもマードックだったし、『タイムズ』紙に賞金ゲームを導入したり王室のゴシップ記事を掲載したりして高級紙と大衆紙の区別を曖昧にし、有名人の私生活に土足で踏み込むパパラッチをはびこらせたのも彼だった。

『サン』はまた、排外主義的で品のない論調でも知られている。アラブ人のテロリストを"アラブのドブネズミ"と呼び、ゲイの人々を"ホモ"と嘲笑する。フォークランド紛争が勃発した1982年には、アルゼンチンの戦艦"ジェネラル・ベルグラノ"の沈没を、"つかまえた"という見出しで祝して世間の顰蹙を買った。"つかまえた"というのは、子どもが鬼ごっこで鬼をつかまえたときに使う表現であり、数百名にのぼる10代の徴集兵が命を落とした事件を語るに適切な言葉とはとうてい言えなかった。

マードックは世論に絶大な影響力を持っている。サッチャー元首相が3度選挙で勝つことができたのも、『サン』(1日400万部の売り上げを誇る)紙の支持が得られたことが大きかったと考えられている。1997年に『サン』が保守党支持をとりやめたことが、ブレアがほぼ20年ぶりに労働党の首相に就任する一助となった。

そんなマードックも、時には国民の感情を読み誤って行きすぎてしまうことがある。たとえば『サン』は、人気歌手のエルトン・ジョンはゲイだと騒ぎたてて発行部数を落としたことがあった。ヒルズバラのサッカー場で多くの若いサッカーファンが圧死したときも、その事故の責任を安全対策の不備ではなくフーリガンに求めたために、さらに多くの読者を失った。

マードックは、英国人が好んで嫌いたがる人物の1人である。新聞を俗っぽく、のぞき趣味で外国嫌いの物質主義的なメディアに変えたと、英国

aggressively downmarket. It was he who introduced topless models to *The Sun*, and who initiated games with cash prizes and gossip about the royal family in *The Times*, blurring the distinction between the quality and mass-market newspapers, and setting off the boom in *paparrazzi* intrusion into the private lives of the famous.

The Sun is also distinguished by a nasty jingoistic streak. Arab terrorists, for instance, are referred to as "Arab rats," while homosexuals are derided as "poofs." During the Falklands War in 1982, the sinking of the Argentine ship *General Belgrano* was celebrated with the notorious headline "GOTCHA" (got you). This is what children say when they catch each other playing tag, but it was hardly appropriate to mark an event in which hundreds of teenage conscripts were killed.

Murdoch has great power to influence public opinion. The support of *The Sun* (with its 4 million daily sales) was regarded as a crucial factor in Mrs. Thatcher's three election victories. And the withdrawal of that support in 1997 contributed to Blair becoming the first Labour prime minister in nearly twenty years.

Occasionally Murdoch's papers misjudge the public and goes too far. *The Sun* lost circulation, for example, when it ran a campaign attacking the much-liked singer Elton John for his homosexuality. And it lost more readers when it attributed the violent deaths of many young fans at Hillsborough football stadium to hooliganism instead of poor safety procedures.

Murdoch is one of the men that the British love to hate. He is criticised for making the press more vulgar, more intrusive, more xenophobic, and more materialistic. His defence is

人はマードックを批判する。それに対するマードックの反論は明快だ。彼は一部のエリートが大衆に与えるべきだと考えるメディアではなく、大衆が実際に求めるメディアを提供しているだけだというのである。

Q: 英国とアメリカのホームドラマにはどんな違いがあるのか？

アメリカの連続テレビドラマの主人公はたいていの場合、華やかな生活を送る金持ちの権力者である。CBSで13年間にわたって放映され、世界じゅうで2億人が観たと言われる『ダラス』も、テキサスの牧場に住む石油長者一家の物語だった。

これに比べて英国のホームドラマは、裕福とは言えないごく普通の人々の生活がテーマになっている。英国の最長寿番組『コロネーション・ストリート』も、さえないテラスハウスが建ち並ぶマンチェスターの架空の通りに暮らす人々の日常生活を描いたものである。エピソードの大半は、豪華マンションの最上階に位置する重役会議室やプールサイドとは似ても似つかない地元のパブ、"ローヴァーズ・リターン"で展開する。

『イースト・エンダーズ』という、『コロネーション・ストリート』を英国南部の住人向けに焼き直したようなテレビドラマも労働者階級の暮らしを描いており、ロンドンのイーストエンドを舞台にしている。このドラマは麻薬や"安全でないセックス"などの現代社会が抱える問題をストーリーに織り込むことによって、『コロネーション・ストリート』とは一線を画そうとしている。

どちらの番組も絶大な人気を博しており、英国の人口の3分の1以上にあたる2000万人を超える人々がこれらの番組を観たこともあった。しかし、

simple. He is just giving the public what the public wants, not what the elite thinks it should get!

Q: How are British and American soap operas different?

American soap operas are generally about rich and powerful people living glamorous lives. For example, CBS's *Dallas*, the most successful soap ever, that ran for thirteen years reaching a global audience of 200 million, told the story of a family of oil tycoons living on a ranch in Texas.

British soap operas, by contrast, deal with the ordinary lives of typical, not very well-off people. *Coronation Street*, a soap opera that is also Britain's longest-running TV program, depicts the everyday life of the inhabitants of a fictional street of grimy terraced houses in Manchester. Most of the action, far from taking place in sleek penthouses, paneled board-rooms, or at the poolside, takes place at the "Rover's Return," the local pub.

East Enders, a kind of *Coronation Street* for the Southern market, again depicts working-class life, but this time in London's East End. It attempts to differentiate itself from *Coronation Street* by introducing controversial contemporary issues such as drugs or unprotected sex.

Both these soap operas attract huge audiences, sometimes being watched by over 20 million people, more than one-third of all people in Britain. But however successful they may be at

国内でどれほど人気があったとしても、英国のテレビドラマは地域性が強すぎるため、海外市場に進出するのは困難である。なにしろ『イースト・エンダーズ』がアメリカで放映された時には、ロンドン訛りの英語の語彙集を、あらかじめ視聴者に配布しなければならなかったほどだったのだ。

最近では『ネイバーズ』や『ホーム・アンド・アウェイ』などのドラマがオーストラリアから輸入され、テレビを通じて他人の生活を疑似体験する機会はますます増えている。

Q: 英国でもっとも成功したミュージシャンは？

英国が多くのポップスターを生みだしてきたことについては、すでに述べたとおりである。ポップミュージックの月刊誌『Q』の1998年8月号に、英国のロックスター100人が資産順に掲載されていた。上位10人を見てみよう。

1位にランクされているのは、5億ポンド（2位の3倍以上）の資産を持つ元ビートルズのメンバー、ポール・マッカートニーである。皮肉なことに、マッカートニーの富の大半はビートルズの楽曲からの印税収入ではなく、彼が買いとった曲の著作権収入によっている。マッカートニーは『ハッピー・バースデイ・トゥ・ユー』の著作権まで所有しているのだ。第2位は、バンドのメンバーと儲けを分け合う必要がないことが有利に働いているのか、ソロ歌手のエルトン・ジョンがランクされている。1960年代初頭以来ローリング・ストーンズを率いて巨額の富を築いてきたミック・ジャガーは、1億2500万ポンドで3位につけている。4位はフィル・コリンズで、5位がデイビッド・ボウイだ。キース・リチャーズは、ストーンズのすべての曲をミック・ジャガーと共作しているにもかかわらず6位にとどまり、そ

home, British soap operas are far too local in flavor to achieve any success in export markets. When *East Enders* was shown in the United States, a glossary explaining Cockney idioms had to be provided in advance to viewers !

Recently the opportunities to live vicariously through soap operas have been further increased with imports from Australia such as *Neighbours* and *Home and Away.*

Q: Who are the most successful British pop stars?

We have already seen that the U.K. has produced more than its fair share of pop superstars. The August 1998 edition of *Q*, the monthly pop music magazine, published a list of the 100 richest British rock'n'roll stars in Britain. Let's have a look at the top ten.

At number one with a fortune of £500 million (over three times as large as his nearest rival) was ex-Beatle, Paul McCartney. Ironically, most of McCartney's wealth comes not from royalties on the Beatles' songs that he wrote, but from song rights that he bought. He even owns the rights to "Happy Birthday to You." Elton John, who, as a solo-performer, obviously benefits from not having to split his earnings with any band members, came in second. Mick Jagger, who has been earning large sums as a Rolling Stone since the early 1960s, was third with £125 million. At number four was Phil Collins, and David Bowie took the number five slot. Keith Richards, despite being co-writer of all the Stones' material with Mick Jagger, only came in at number six, some

の資産はミック・ジャガーより2500万ポンドも少ない1億ポンドと推定されている。このささやかな不足額は、おそらくは1970年代に金のかかるヘロインを常用したことと、そのために全身の血を入れ替えるという途方もない治療を受けたことによるのだろう。

ソロ歌手のスティングは、アイルランドのグループU2のメンバーとともに7位につけている。9位は元ビートルズのメンバー（映画のプロデューサーとしても成功している）ジョージ・ハリスンで、トップテンの最後を締めくくるのは、精力的にコンサートツアーをこなすブルースギタリスト、エリック・クラプトンである。

英国のポップスターが巨万の富を築くためには、3つの条件を満たす必要があるようだ。まず第1に、国内市場で売れるだけに留まらず世界的な成功をおさめること。第2に、できるだけたくさんの印税収入を手に入れるために、自分で作った曲を自分で演奏すること。そして最後に、数十年間継続して売れつづけること、である。

Q: ロンドンの劇場はなぜこんなに人気があるのか？

ロンドンの劇場は、首都経済のなかでもっとも景気のいい業界の1つである。ロンドン劇場協会のホームページを開けば、ロンドン市内の50ヵ所に及ぶ劇場のリストを見ることができる。しかもこれらはいずれも場末の芝居小屋ではなく、歌舞伎座級の一流劇場なのだ。

ロンドンの劇場の大半はウェストエンド地区にあり、とくにシャフツベリー・アベニューという通りに集中して建っている。そのほとんどが、大英帝国の繁栄が頂点に達したエドワード7世時代に創設されたものだ。

£25 million less wealthy than Jagger with a fortune estimated at £100 million. This little deficit can probably be attributed to his rather expensive heroin habit in the 1970s, and the extraordinary treatments—total blood transfusions—it necessitated!

Sting, another solo singer-songwriter, was at seventh place, equal with the the members of the Irish band U2. Bringing up the end of the top ten was ex-Beatle (and successful film producer) George Harrison, followed by blues guitarist and indefatigable tourer Eric Clapton.

There are three criteria for achieving enormous wealth as a British pop star. First, you need to be successful not just in the domestic market but on a worldwide basis. Second, you should be performing music you have composed yourself so you can maximize your royalty rate. Third, you should be successful for several decades in a row!

Q: Why is the London Theatre so successful?

The London Theatre is one of the most flourishing sectors of the capital's economy. A visit to the official website of the Society of London Theatre provides a list of fifty venues in London, and these are not smokey little dives but full-size Kabuki-zas!

Most of the theaters in London are found in the West End, with a particularly high concentration around Shaftesbury Avenue. The majority date from the Edwardian period, the high-water mark of imperial prosperity.

　観光客が大挙してロンドンに押し寄せるように
なると、劇場は財布の紐の固い英国人よりも、金
遣いの荒い外国人客をターゲットにして利益をあ
げるようになった。もちろん、観光客はアメリカ人
も含めてイギリス英語の理解に難がある。近年ロ
ンドンでミュージカルの人気が高いのはそのため
である。初めて大ヒットしたミュージカルは、1972
年から8年間にわたって上演されたアンドリュー・
ロイド・ウェーバーのロックオペラ、『ジーザス・ク
ライスト・スーパー・スター』だった。ロイド・ウェ
ーバーはウェストエンドのスピルバーグとなり、彼
の作品は最長上演記録を持つ上位5作品のうち4
つを占めている。

　とはいえ、ミュージカルは製作に莫大な経費が
かかり、万一失敗すれば興行主は身を滅ぼしかね
ない。そのために、ミュージカル以外の従来の演
劇もいまだ健在である。アガサ・クリスティの推理
劇『ねずみとり』は上演46年目に突入し、やはり記
録保持作品となっている。

　インテリ好みの演劇に目を向ければ、シェイクス
ピア作品を熱心に上演する劇場がロンドンには3
ヵ所もあり(英国国立劇場、バービカン劇場、グロ
ーブ座)、いつでもシェイクスピア劇を観ることが
できる。ロンドンの劇場ではまた、ピーター・オト
ゥール(『アラビアのロレンス』)やジェレミー・アイ
アンズ(『運命の逆転』)ら、世界的にその名を知ら
れた英国人俳優によるシェイクスピア劇を鑑賞す
ることもできる。

　英国人はなぜこれほど演劇に長けているのだ
ろうか?　その理由の一端が教育にあるのは間違
いなさそうだ。数字や事実の暗記に重点を置く日
本の教育は、有能で役に立ち、技術者かサラリー
マンになることだけを夢見る子どもたちを育てる
ことを目的としている。一方で英国の教育は、感

Mass tourism has made it more profitable for theaters to appeal to the free-spending foreign audience than to the tight-fisted domestic audience. Of course, tourists—including Americans—have some difficulty with the English language. This accounts for the recent success of musicals in London. The first massive musical hit was Andrew Lloyd-Webber's rock opera, *Jesus Christ Superstar*, which ran for eight years from 1972. Lloyd Webber has gone on to become the Spielberg of the West End, holding four of the top five records for longest running production.

Musicals, however, are very expensive to put on and ruinous to the promoters should they fail. Traditional, non-musical theater is therefore holding its own. Agatha Christie's murder mystery, *The Mousetrap*—now in its forty-sixth year—is the record-holder here.

At the high-brow end of things, Shakespeare is always well represented on the London stage with three venues (National Theatre, Barbican, and Globe) dedicated to his works. It is still possible to catch internationally famous British actors, such as Peter O'Toole (*Lawrence of Arabia*), or Jeremy Irons (*Reversal of Fortune*) performing Shakespeare on the London stage.

Why are the British so good at theater? Education must have something to do with it. Japanese education—concentrating on facts, numbers, memorization—aims to make a child functional and useful, lusting only to be an engineer or a salaryman. British education—concentrating on the cultivation of sensibility and the powers of self-expression—produces

性を育んで表現力を身につけさせることを重視しており、面白みはあってもあまり役に立たない、芸術家になることだけを夢見る人間を大量に生みだしている。つまり、英国は役者志願者の宝庫なのである。

英国の俳優の優秀さは疑問の余地のないところであり、真の芸術作品を目指してつくられたハリウッド映画には、かならず英国の俳優が起用されていることも興味深い事実だ。レイフ・ファインズ、リーアム・ニーソン、ベン・キングズレーの3人を起用したスピルバーグ監督の『シンドラーのリスト』は、その好例と言えるだろう。

Q: 英国は推理小説発祥の地か？

世界初の推理小説は、アメリカ人のエドガー・アラン・ポーが1841年に発表した短編、『モルグ街の殺人事件』だと誰もが認めているが、推理小説という分野が市民権を獲得して発展したのは、3人の英国人作家の功績によるところ大である。

その3人のうち1人は、1887年にシャーロック・ホームズを生みだしたサー・アーサー・コナン・ドイル（1859〜1930）である。ホームズの人気はすさまじく、ドイルは（本格的歴史ロマンを書きたいがために）1894年にいったんはホームズの息の根を止めたものの、読者の強い要望によってしぶしぶ彼を復活させねばならなかったほどだった。鳥打ち帽をかぶりパイプをくわえたシャーロック・ホームズは、ミッキー・マウス並みに世界的に知られている。"基本だよ、ワトソン君"などのホームズのセリフも、いまや決まり文句として日常英語でも使われているし、第2次世界大戦中には、ホームズはユニバーサル・スタジオ製作のシリーズでナチスとも戦った。

large quantities of ornamental, but slightly useless people, eager only to be artistic. Hence, the existence of a large talent pool.

The quality of British actors is beyond question, and it is amusing to note that any Hollywood production that aspires to be serious art invariably has a British cast. Spielberg's *Schindler's List*—starring Ralph Fiennes, Liam Neeson, and Ben Kingsley—is a classic example of this phenomenon.

Q: Did crime fiction originate in Britain?

Although the first work of detective fiction is agreed to be *The Murders in the Rue Morgue*, an 1841 short story by the American Edgar Allan Poe, the genre was popularized and developed by three British authors.

The first of these was Sir Arthur Conan Doyle (1859– 1930), who created Sherlock Holmes in 1887. Holmes was so popular that even though his author (who wanted to write serious historical romances) killed him off in 1894, public demand forced him to engineer his return. Sherlock Holmes, with his deer-stalker hat and pipe, is regularly cited as one of the most widely recognized characters in the world on a par with Mickey Mouse. Some of Holmes's famous lines, such as, "Elementary, my dear Watson," have become popular idioms in the English language, and during World War II Sherlock Holmes even fought the Nazis in a Universal Studios' series!

　2人目は"ミステリーの女王"と讃えられる多作な作家、アガサ・クリスティ（1891〜1976）である。クリスティの推理小説は世界最高の売り上げを記録し、総販売部数は（クリスティは78もの作品を執筆した）20億部と推定されている。クリスティが創りだした探偵のなかで一番の人気者は、口髭をはやした小太りのベルギー人エルキュール・ポワロと、上品な老嬢ミス・マープルだろう。シャーロック・ホームズがロンドン（"大英帝国の怠け者のらくら者がこぞって集まる、かの偉大な汚物だめ"）を中心に活躍したのに比べて、アガサ・クリスティの小説はカントリーハウスを舞台にして犯人を推理するものが大半である。

　クリスティの小説の基本形は次のとおりだ。週末に何人かの客がカントリーハウスに招待される。そのうち1人が図書室で死体で発見される。そのとき探偵が現れるか、もしくは偶然探偵も招待客の1人である。滞在客1人1人が、それぞれの立場で事件を説明する。探偵は彼らの証言に食い違いを発見し、殺人者の仮面が暴かれる。とまあ、こんな具合である。アメリカ人はこのようなきわめて不自然でブルジョワ趣味の小説に反発し、ハードボイルドという分野を作った。

　英国が生んだ推理作家3人組の最後を締めくくるのは、殺しのライセンスと007のコードネームを持つ洗練された秘密諜報員、ジェームズ・ボンドを創りだしたイアン・フレミングである。ジェームズ・ボンドのシリーズは、大衆小説の素材にセックスと暴力と一流ブランドの商品名（ボンドはロレックスをはじめ、ベントレーを駆り、ドンペリニョンを飲む）を織り込むことにより、昨今の空港の待合室に欠くことのできない"ショッピングとセックス"をテーマにした小説の基礎を築いた。

　英国の歴史はありとあらゆるものの衰退の歴史

The second author was the prolific Agatha Christie (1890–1976), nicknamed the "Queen of Crime." She is the world's best-selling writer of detective fiction, and her books (she wrote 78 in total!) are estimated to have sold two billion copies!! Her most popular crime-fighting creations are Hercule Poirot, a plump, mustachioed Belgian, and Miss Marple, a genteel, elderly spinster. While Sherlock Holmes' activities were centered on London ("that great cesspool into which all the loungers and idlers of the Empire are irresistably drained"), Agatha Christie's novels were chiefly whodunnits that took place at country houses.

The basic formula was: a number of guests gather for the weekend; one of said guests is found dead in the library; a detective appears or happens to be at the party; everyone present gives their account of events; the detective finds an inconsistency and the killer is unmasked. American hard-boiled novels were a reaction to this highly artificial and very bourgeois genre.

The final writer in this British triumvirate is Ian Fleming, creator of James Bond 007, the suave secret agent with the license to kill. James Bond books introduced sex, violence, and brand names (Bond wore a Rolex, drove a Bentley, drank Dom Perignon) into the best-seller mix, thus laying the foundations for the "shopping and fucking" literature of present-day airport lounges.

The history of Britain is the history of universal decline,

であり、推理小説もまた例外ではない。歴史家の
E・J・ホブズオウムは "近年英国の有力な輸出商
品となった推理小説は、アメリカ式のスリラーに圧
倒されて影響力を失った" と、1968年の時点で述
べていた。

Q: 英国の映画産業が近年勢いを取り戻したのはなぜか？

　英国映画の人気復活を象徴するのは、エディン
バラに住むヘロイン中毒者の日常生活という、とう
てい大衆受けしそうにないテーマを選びながら
も、7200万ドルの収益をあげた『トレインスポッティ
ング』だろう。製作費はわずか350万ドルだった
というから、1996年に製作された映画のなかでも
っとも高い利益率をあげた作品ではなかったろう
か。同じ年に公開されたマイク・リーの『秘密と
嘘』はカンヌで賞をとったし、『イングリッシュ・ペ
イシェント』は9部門でオスカーを受賞した。

　英国は昔から優秀な映画人を数多く輩出してき
た。ハリウッドを席巻したチャーリー・チャップリ
ンもアルフレッド・ヒッチコックもデビッド・リーン
も、みんな英国人である。現在でも、ショーン・コ
ネリー、ジェレミー・アイアンズ、ダニエル・デイ・
ルイス、アンソニー・ホプキンス、リーアム・ニーソ
ンといった実力派俳優や、エイドリアン・ライン
(『ナインハーフ』)、リドリー・スコット(『ブレードラ
ンナー』『エイリアン』)、トニー・スコット(『トップガ
ン』『トゥルー・ロマンス』)などの監督が活躍して
いる。映画産業(およびその他の産業)で英国人
に欠けているものは商才、つまり資本を募り、製
作したものを売り出す能力である。

　1970年代初頭に英国経済が崩壊すると、映画監
督たちは運命に弄ばれて惨めな暮らしを送る哀

and detective fiction is no exception. As early as 1968, the historian E. J. Hobsawm commented that the "late but powerful British export has lost its hold, conquered by the American-patterned thriller."

Q: What has caused the recent revival in the British film industry?

The film which symbolizes the recent revival in the British film industry is *Trainspotting*, which, despite its less-than-promising theme of the everyday life of Edinburgh heroin addicts, grossed US$72 million. Since its production costs were only $3.5 million, it achieved the highest profit to cost ratio of any film in 1996. In the same year Mike Leigh's *Secrets and Lies* won an award at Cannes, and *The English Patient* won nine Oscars.

Britain has always had film talent. After all, Hollywood greats, like Charlie Chaplin, Alfred Hitchcock, and David Lean were all British. More recently there have been actors of the caliber of Sean Connery, Jeremy Irons, Daniel Day-Lewis, Anthony Hopkins, and Liam Neeson, as well as directors like Adrian Lyne (*Nine-and-a-Half Weeks*), Ridley Scott (*Bladerunner, Alien*) and Tony Scott (*Top Gun, True Romance*). What Britain was lacking in the movie business (as in any other business) was commercial know-how—the ability to raise capital and then to market what it had made.

The general collapse of the British economy in the early 1970s meant that directors began to produce films that pre-

れな人々にあふれた国家という、現在の英国の姿を忠実に描いた作品を撮りはじめた。こうした映画は監督の道義心を満足させると同時に、国内外の映画ファンを辟易させることに成功した。写実的な作品群の一方で、大英帝国の栄光を美化した『炎のランナー』や『眺めのいい部屋』に代表される、特定の時代を舞台にした作品群が生まれた。一方は自己憐憫に浸り、他方は過去の思い出に浸るという、奇妙な二極化が進んだのである。

しかしここに来て、映画産業に2つの明るい材料が現れた。1つには映画館への入場者数が増加し、1996年には1983年の倍になったことである。そして2つ目は、多くの映画が英国で製作されるようになり、1992年にはわずか47本だったのが1995年には78本に、さらに1996年には128本にと驚異的な伸びを見せていることだ。製作数が一挙に増えたのは、英米共同製作(『ビーン』がその一例)の作品や、純粋なアメリカ作品(『ミッション・インポシブル』や『フィフス・エレメント』)が英国で製作されはじめたことにある。英国のほうが人件費が安く、芸術的才能に恵まれた人材にも事欠かないことから、アメリカ人はパインウッドやリーヴズデンにある第一級の映画撮影所に魅力を感じている。

英国映画が現在の勢いを保ちつづけることができるかどうかは、まだわからない。英国という国家そのものが持つ、失敗しようとする意志の強さには侮れないものがあるからだ。悲観主義者たちは、『フル・モンティ』は英国の俳優を起用して英国で撮影されたが米国資本だっただの、海外の映画会社が英国で映画を撮るのはポンドが安値に傾いているときだけだだの、『トレインスポッティング』は商業的には成功したかもしれないが麻薬中毒を美化しており道徳的に見て問題があるだのと、早くも熱心に指摘しはじめている。

＊統計の数値は英国映画研究所発行『Film & Television Handbook』1998年版より

sented Britain truthfully, as a derelict country full of sad victims of fate leading grim lives. This may have made the directors feel morally worthy, but the films successfully repelled both domestic and national audiences. These works of social realism were balanced by period dramas such as *Chariots of Fire* or *Room with a View*, which presented an idealized version of imperial Britain. There was a grotesque polarization, with one school drowning in self-pity and the other in nostalgia.

Recently there have been two positive trends in the movie industry. First, cinema admissions have risen, with the 1996 figure being double that of 1983. Second, the number of films made in Britain has shot up—from 47 in 1992, to 78 in 1995, and an astonishing 128 in 1996. This surge is due to an increase in the number of U.S. / U.K. co-productions (such as *Bean*), or purely U.S. productions (like *Mission: Impossible* or *The Fifth Element*). The Americans are attracted to Britain because of the world-class studios at Pinewood and Leavesden, because labor is cheaper than in the U.S., and because there is plenty of creative talent.

It remains to be seen whether this renaissance of the British cinema will be able to sustain its momentum. The collective will to failure may be too strong. Already the Jeremiahs are eagerly pointing out that *The Full Monty*, though made in Britain with British actors, was American-financed; that foreign productions will be made in Britain only if the pound is weak; that *Trainspotting* may have succeeded commerically, but by glamorizing drug-abuse, failed morally etc.

*Figures ftrom BFI Film & Television Handbook 1998

Q: 英国のテレビはチャンネルがいくつあり、それぞれどんな違いがあるのか？

　　テレビを観るのは英国でもっとも一般的な"活動"で、国民は週に平均24時間テレビを観ている。ビデオも人気があり、ビデオを所有する人の割合はアメリカや日本よりも英国のほうが高いほどだ。

　　地上波放送は、BBC1、BBC2、ITV、チャンネル4、チャンネル5の5つのチャンネルから成っている。BBC1とBBC2は受信料によって運営されている公共チャンネルで、広告収入は皆無である。一方のITV、チャンネル4、チャンネル5の各チャンネルは民間放送で、コマーシャルや事業活動から収入を得ている。

　　もっとも高い視聴率を誇るのはITVで、平均で35パーセントの視聴者を獲得している。続いてBBC1が32.5パーセントで、その他の地上波チャンネル（BBC2では、あまり大衆向けでない教養番組を放映し、一方チャンネル5では、三流のホームドラマや安っぽい映画、ソフトポルノ映画を放映）や、受信料の必要なケーブルテレビ／衛星放送の視聴率は極端に低い。

　　視聴者が好んで観るのは単発ドラマや連続ホームドラマ、スポーツ中継、そしてニュース番組である。もっとも、スポーツ中継の多くは多額の放映権料を支払うことのできる衛星放送局へ移行しはじめている。ルパート・マードックが経営するニューズ・コーポレーションは、先頃サッカーチームのマンチェスター・ユナイテッドを買収する用意があることを表明し、うまくいけば、みずからが経営するスカイTVをとおしてマンチェスター・ユナイテッドの試合を全世界に向けて独占放映する権利を手に入れる。予算の限られたBBCやその他の国内

Q: **How many TV channels are there in Britain and how do they differ from each other?**

Watching TV is the most popular "activity" in Britain, with people watching an average of 24 hours per week. Videos are also popular, and ownership of video recorders is actually higher in the U.K. than in either the U.S. or Japan.

There are five terrestrial channels. BBC 1, BBC 2, ITV, Channel 4, and Channel 5. BBC 1 and BBC 2 are public channels funded by the television license fee, and have no advertising income. ITV, Channel 4, and Channel 5 are commercial channels that derive all their income from commercials, or commercial ventures.

ITV has the highest share of the TV audience, with an average of just over 35 percent. BBC 1 has a 32.5 percent share, then there is a big drop to the other terrestrial channels (BBC2 shows less mass-market, more intellectual fare, while Channel 5 shows 3rd rate soap operas and soft focus, soft porn films) and to cable/satellite TV for which subscription fees must be paid.

The shows that draw the highest audiences are dramas, soap operas, sporting events, and the news. Many sporting events, however, have now shifted to satellite TV because it is prepared to pay huge fees for exclusive broadcasting rights. Rupert Murdoch's News Corporation recently announced his intention to buy the Manchester United soccer team. The deal would give him exclusive rights to beam their matches around the world on his SkyTV network. How the BBC with its limited budget, or even domestic independent channels, can compete with multinational entertainment conglomerates is a difficult question.

の放送局が、娯楽産業界に君臨する多国籍企業と互角に渡り合っていけるかどうかはむずかしいところだろう。

英国人は自国のテレビ番組こそ世界一だと自負し、誇りを持っている。だがJ.G.バラード（『クラッシュ』や『太陽の帝国』の著者）の見解は違うようだ。バラードは、テレビ番組の質の高さこそがテレビを有害なものにしていると考えている。「テレビ番組は良質であってはならない。テレビ番組が優れているというのは、世界一おいしいジャンクフードがあると自慢するのと同じことである……この国が衰退したのは、テレビ番組がクズではないという事実によるところが大きい……国民は家にこもってひたすらテレビに見入る……映画に出かけたり本を読んだりする者は1人もいない。まさに文化の死である」

＊統計の数値は英国映画研究所発行『Film & Television Handbook』1998年版より

Q: BBCはどこが特別なのか？

BBCは1922年に英国放送社として設立されたが、勅許を得て1927年に英国放送協会となった。当初はラジオ局だったが、1936年にテレビ放送を開始した。初めは独占企業だったが、1955年からは民間テレビ局との競争を、1973年からは民間ラジオ局との競争を余儀なくされてきた。運営費は受信料のみで賄われている。

BBCはテレビとラジオの国内放送だけでなく、"ワールドサービス"という国際短波放送を実施し、事実を客観的に伝えることで高い評価を受けている。最近ではワーナーのCNNに対抗すべく、"BBCワールド"という国際テレビ放送も開始した。

The British are proud of their TV, which they regard as the best in the world. But J. G. Ballard (author of *Crash* and *Empire of the Sun*) has a novel point of view. He thinks that the very quality of the TV is what makes it harmful: "Television *should not* be good. It's like saying you've got the best junk food in the world. . . The decline of this country is largely attributable to the fact that our television isn't trash. . . People sit at home and watch TV. . . nobody goes to the movies, nobody reads books. It's the death of a culture."

＊Figures from BFI Film & Television Handbook 1998

Q: What is so special about the BBC?

The BBC was founded in 1922 as the British Broadcasting Company, but received a royal charter as the British Broadcasting Corporation in 1927. Originally a radio station, the BBC branched into television in 1936. At first it was a monopoly, but came up against competition from commercial TV broadcasters in 1955, and from commercial radio stations in 1973. It is funded entirely by license fees.

In addition to domestic TV and radio stations, the BBC has the World Service, a short-wave radio service that is broadcast around the world and is highly respected because of its commitment to telling the truth objectively. Recently the BBC have also set up BBC World, a global TV Channel designed to compete with Warner's CNN.

BBCの初代総局長を務めたリース卿は、厳格なことで知られていた。ラジオのニュースキャスターは、ニュースを読むにあたってタキシードに身を包まねばならず、"容認発音"で話すことが義務づけられた。もっとも、最近では規制は和らいでいる。地方訛りも、もはやタブーではなくなった。それでも番組の品質はいまも保たれている。

国際的に高い評価を受けているBBCも、つねに新たな問題に直面してきた。公共放送であるにもかかわらず、BBCをもっとも強烈に攻撃するのは政府であった。サッチャー政権時代には、"理想主義者や社会主義者"に牛耳られ、"自由競争の世界から不自然に保護された独占企業"と嘲笑された。これはもちろん、英国の治安当局や政治家に批判的な番組を製作するBBCに、政治家が腹をたてていたことを意味している。

放送業界が自由化されたのは、"独立心が旺盛すぎて"政府に従わないBBCに対する制裁だったと、一般には理解されている。自由化以来BBCは、巨額の資金にものを言わせてスポーツ中継の放映権を買いあさる衛星放送局と張り合わねばならなくなった。大衆受けするスポーツ中継の大半を他局に奪われる事態になったら、格式あるBBCも弱体化するのではないかと懸念されている。

Q: 英国はどんな文豪を生んだのか？

世界じゅうで愛され親しまれている古典的な文学作品の多くが、英国から生まれている。それらの古典作品を執筆した文豪の筆頭はもちろん、36の戯曲を書き、『リア王』『ハムレット』『オセロ』『マクベス』の4代悲劇が代表作とされるシェイクスピア（1564〜1616）である。『リア王』と『マクベス』は、黒澤明が舞台を日本に置き換えて映画化している。

The first manager of the BBC, Lord Reith, was famous for his strictness. Radio newscasters had to dress in dinner jackets to read the news, and only "received pronunciation" was acceptable. In recent years, however, things have relaxed. Regional accents are no longer taboo, but the quality of programming remains extremely high.

The BBC, despite its international reputation, is having to face new challenges all the time. Some of the most fierce attacks on it have—ironically, since it is a public broadcasting service—been mounted by the goverment. Mrs. Thatcher went so far as to replace the old style management—who believed that objective and impartial reporting was their sacred duty— with placemen who dutifully reported events as the government wished them to be reported.

This ideological decay—coupled with endless restructurings designed to make the BBC more commercial and efficient—has led to much upheaval within the organisation. But there are also threats from the outside, the greatest of which is satellite television. In the area of sport the BBC, with its restricted budget, is easily outbid for broadcasting rights by specialist channels such as SKYTV, and is now no longer able to offer coverage of many of the major sporting events that are so important a part of British life.

Q: What great writers has Britain produced?

Many literary classics that are read and loved all around the world come from Britain. The natural starting point is, of course, Shakespeare (1564–1616) who wrote a total of thirty-six plays, of which the four tragedies *King Lear*, *Hamlet*, *Othello* and *Macbeth* are regarded as his greatest masterpieces. *King Lear* and *Macbeth* were both remade as movies in a Japanese context by Akira Kurosawa.

その翌世紀の代表的な文学者と言えば、ピューリタン革命において議会勢力を率いたオリヴァー・クロムウェルの秘書官を務め、宗教叙事詩『失楽園』を書いたジョン・ミルトン（1608〜74）だ。宗教的な主題を持ち、重苦しすぎるミルトンの作品は、現在では大学などの学校で読まれるのみとなっている。

18世紀になり、議会制民主主義に移行した英国は、小説を読んで暇を潰す必要のある貿易成金を生みだした。1719年にダニエル・デフォーが難破船の船乗りの物語『ロビンソン・クルーソー』を発表し、1726年にはジョナサン・スウィフトの『ガリバー旅行記』が出版された。

英国が世界最強の軍事力と経済力を誇る大国になった19世紀初頭には、小説家サー・ウォルター・スコット（印税収入で城と船を買った）と詩人のバイロン卿という、世界初のベストセラー作家が誕生した。

ビクトリア女王の時代に入ると、チャールズ・ディケンズが分冊形式の小説『ピクウィック・ペイパーズ』を発表し、弱冠24歳にして成功をおさめた。ディケンズはその後『オリバー・トウィスト』『大いなる遺産』『二都物語』などを次々に発表した。ディケンズも商売に鼻が利き、アメリカでみずからの作品の朗読会を開いたり（女性の聴衆が感極まって失神したという）、海賊版が出回るのを防ぐために英国とアメリカで同日出版したりした。

19世紀後半には、ロバート・ルイス・スティーヴンソンの『ジキル博士とハイド氏』やブラム・ストーカーの『吸血鬼ドラキュラ』などの、どちらかと言えばあまり文学的でない大衆受けする作品が人気を集めた。この傾向は20世紀に入っても、コナ

The leading literary figure of the next century was John Milton (1608–74), who penned the religious epic *Paradise Lost* in addition to acting as secretary to Oliver Cromwell, the leader of the Parliamentary forces in the civil war. Now the reading of Milton—whose religious subject matter is extremely austere—is limited to schools and universities.

Come the eighteenth century and Britain, with its parliamentary democracy, was developing a trade-enriched bourgeoisie who needed to be entertained with novels. In 1719, Daniel Defoe published *Robinson Crusoe*, the story of a shipwrecked sailor, and in 1726 Jonathan Swift's *Gulliver's Travels* appeared.

In the early nineteenth century, as Britain's became the world's preeminent military and economic power, it produced the first ever "bestseller" writers in the form of the novelist Sir Walter Scott (who was able to build himself a castle and buy a yacht on his royalties) and the poet Lord Byron.

Entering the reign of Queen Victoria, Charles Dickens leapt to fame at the age of twenty-four with his serial *The Pickwick Papers*. He went on to produce a series of classic novels including *Oliver Twist*, *Great Expectations* and *A Tale of Two Cities*. He, too, had a good nose for business, conducting readings of his work in the U.S. (during which women in the audience fainted from emotion!) and publishing his work on the same day in the U.K. and U.S. to minimize the risk of pirating.

The late eighteenth century saw a surge in the number of less literary, more popular works, such as Robert Louis Stevenson's *Dr. Jekyll and Mr. Hyde* and Bram Stoker's *Dracula*. This trend continued into the twentieth century with the works of Conan Doyle and Agatha Christie. Meanwhile

ン・ドイルやアガサ・クリスティなどの作品に引き継がれた。一方で純文学作品の創作の場はアイルランドへと移り、劇作家ジョージ・バーナード・ショー（1925年ノーベル賞受賞）、ジェイムス・ジョイス、そしてサミュエル・ベケット（1969年ノーベル賞受賞）が、新たな形式と内容を持つ実験的な作品に取り組んだ。

19世紀には、ビクトリア朝時代に特有の上品ぶった道徳観のおかげで、性は文学の世界から閉めだされていた。英国の小説家、D・H・ロレンスはこの潮流にたったひとりで立ち向かい、1928年に『チャタレイ夫人の恋人』を発表したが、悪名高きこの作品はその後30年以上にわたって英国で発禁処分にあった。20世紀の英国文学は、少数の賞賛すべき例外（イヴリン・ウォーの『スクープ』やアンソニー・バージェスの『時計じかけのオレンジ』など）をのぞけば視野の狭い作品ばかりで、休眠状態に入っている。階級へのこだわり、社会経済の衰退、金儲けの是非、ロンドンとオックスフォード対北部といったテーマは、人類が抱える普遍的なテーマとは言い難い。

それでも、英国は今世紀の偉大な作家たちにわずかながらも関わってきたと主張することはできるかもしれない。『ロリータ』を書いたウラジミール・ナボコフは、ケンブリッジ大学に通ったし、探偵小説を芸術の域にまで高めたレイモンド・チャンドラーは、ロンドン郊外のダリッチで教育を受けた。

最後はJ・G・バラードの言葉で締めくくることにしよう。「英国には文学作品があり余っている……この500年間というもの、われわれは天才作家を大量に生みだしてきた……英国人は、もう小説には飽き飽きしているのかもしれない。私たちにはこれ以上小説は必要ないのである」

the production of serious literature had moved over to Ireland, where the playwright George Bernard Shaw (Nobel Prize, 1925), and the novelists James Joyce and Samuel Beckett (Nobel Prize, 1969) experimented with new content and forms.

In the nineteenth century Victorian prudery had kept sex off the printed page. The English novelist D. H. Lawrence attempted to reverse this singlehandedly, achieving notoriety for *Lady Chatterley's Lover*, which was banned in Britain for over thirty years after its first publication in 1928. However, with a few honorable exceptions (like Evelyn Waugh's *Scoop*, and Anthony Burgess' *Clockwork Orange*) twentieth-century British literature is characterized by torpid parochialism. Obsessions with class, chronic economic and social decay, the rights and wrongs of money-making, London and Oxford versus the North—these are hardly universal themes!

Britain can at least claim tangential relationships to some of the century's great writers. Vladimir Nabokov, the author of *Lolita* attended Cambridge University as an undergraduate, and Raymond Chandler, who raised detective fiction to the level of art, was educated in the London suburb of Dulwich.

Let J. G. Ballard have the last word. "The British have got a surfeit of literature. . . For 500 years we've produced this vast quantity of writers of genius. . . In a sense the British feel we've got enough novels! We don't need any more novels."

Q: 英国の作家は児童文学の分野でも多くの名作を生みだしたか？

貧しい国においては、子どもは家庭の収入を増やし、両親の老後の生活を保障する年金制度代わりに大量に生産される。一方豊かな国では、経済的な目的ではなく感傷的な目的のために生産される。子どもは抱っこし、着飾らせ、誕生日やクリスマスにプレゼント攻めにするための人間ペットなのである。

19世紀から20世紀初頭にかけて、英国は世界一豊かな国家だった。したがって、就寝前に子どもにおとぎ話を読んで聞かせたがる中流階級の家庭数も世界一だった。需要があるところには供給が生まれる。ルイス・キャロルが『不思議の国のアリス』と『鏡の国のアリス』を、それぞれ1865年と1871年に発表すると、たちまちベストセラーになった。ラドヤード・キプリングの『ジャングル・ブック』(1894)、ベアトリックス・ポッターの『ピーター・ラビットのおはなし』(1901)、J・M・バリーの『ピーター・パン』(1904)、A・A・ミルンの『クマのプーさん』(1926)など、一つを除いていまやディズニーの手中に落ちた作品群も同様の成功をおさめた。

英国の児童書に登場するキャラクターが世界じゅうで親しまれるようになったのは、書籍だけでなくビデオやおもちゃなどのありとあらゆる物品を使った抜け目ないマーケティングによるところが大きいと言えるだろう。W・オードリーの"機関車トーマス"、マイケル・ボンドの"パディントン"、レイモンド・ブリッグスの"スノーマン"は、いずれも莫大な版権収入を稼いでいる。『チョコレート工場の秘密』や『おばけ桃の冒険』を書いたロアルド・ダールは、印税収入のおかげで英国一の大富豪になった。

Q: Have British authors produced many children's classics?

In poor countries children are produced in large quantities to increase the family income and serve as the parents' pension plan. In rich countries children are not produced for economic, but for sentimental, purposes. They are human pets, to be cuddled, dressed up, and buried in presents at birthdays and Christmas.

Nineteenth- and early twentieth-century Britain was the richest country in the world. It consequently had the largest number of middle-class families with children demanding to be read bedtime stories. Supply met their demands. Lewis Carroll's *Alice's Adventures in Wonderland* and *Through the Looking Glass* became instant favorites on publication in 1865 and 1871, respectively. The same can be said of Rudyard Kipling's *Jungle Book* (1894), Beatrix Potter's *The Tale of Peter Rabbit* (1901), J. M. Barrie's *Peter Pan* (1904), and A. A. Milne's *Winnie the Pooh* (1926)—all bar one of which have now fallen into the hands of Disney.

Canny marketing has played a big part in the internationalization of British children's characters which exist not just in bookform, but as videos, toys, and 101 forms of merchandising. Rev. W. Audry's *Thomas the Tank Engine*, Michael Bond's *Paddington*, and *Raymong* Briggs' *Snowman* are all licensing goldmines. Roald Dahl, author of *Charley and the Chocolate Factory* and *James and the Giant Peach* became one of the richest men in Britain thanks to royalties from his works.

　子供向けの娯楽作品はいまも続々と誕生している。最近ではニック・パーク監督のアニメーション作品『ウォレスとグルミット』や、BBCの『テレタビーズ』が人気を博している。

The production of children's entertainment continues to flourish in the U.K. Recent successes include Nick Park's *Wallace and Grommitt* animations and the BBC's *Teletubbies*.

飲食

FOOD & DRINK

Q: 英国料理はなぜあんなにまずいのか？

英国料理は驚くほどまずいことで世界的に有名である。英国の料理はほかの国とは違い、地域ごとの特色がなく、懸命に観光に励んだあとでも夕食に名物料理を期待できない英国の食事に、がっかりする観光客は多い。どこへ行っても、想像力のかけらもない代わりばえのしない食事——フィッシュ・アンド・チップス、フライドチキン、ステーキ・アンド・キドニー・パイ、贅沢できる場合はローストビーフ——で満足しなければならないのだ。なお悪いことに、料理はどれもこれも茹ですぎ、焼きすぎである。ローストビーフは焦げてパサパサだし、フィッシュ・アンド・チップスは油でギトギト、もし申し訳程度の野菜が添えられていたとしても、味が抜けるまでくたくたに茹でられている。サラダにはドレッシングがかかっておらず、人間よりもむしろウサギに適した代物。英国人の食事に対する姿勢をもっとも端的に表しているのは、おそらくサンドイッチだろう。食事には栄養が必要だが、五感に歓びを与えるものであってはならないし、社交の場にもなるべきではないのである。英国人と英国料理について考えるにあたっては、磔にされたときにイエス・キリストが示した寛大な態度を見習うのが一番だろう——赦したまえ。彼らは自分がなにをしているかわかっていないのだ！

そんな英国の料理にも、最近はロンドンの金融街“シティ”に集まる儲けすぎの銀行家や投資家の肥える一方の舌に引きずられて、ささやかなルネッサンスが起きている。英国人シェフによる斬新な解釈の伝統英国料理を出す優れたレストランが現れはじめたのである。もっとも、だからと言って一般人の食生活も変化したと考えるのは大きな間違いである。英国ではいまでも、炭水化物主体の

Q: Why is British food so bad?

British food is famous the worldover for being exceptionally bad. Many tourists are disappointed that British food, unlike that of most other countries, does not vary region by region, and consequently there is never any local speciality to look forward to after a hard day's sightseeing. Wherever you go you are forced to content yourself with the same unimaginative meals—fish and chips, fried chicken, steak and kidney pie, or roast beef for the extravagant. To add insult to injury, everything will be overcooked. The roast beef will be brown and dry, the fish and chips will be greasy, and any vegetables that may have slipped in will have been boiled to the point of sodden tastelessness. Salad will be served without dressing in a manner more suited to rabbits than to people. Perhaps it is the sandwich that best encapsulates the British attitude to food. Food should nourish, but it should not provide any sensual delight, nor should it be an occasion for a social gathering. The best way to think about the British and their cooking is to adopt the magnanimous attitude taken by Jesus on the cross:— "Forgive them, for they know not what they do!"

Recently there has been a minor renaissance in British cooking driven by the increasingly luxurious tastes of the over-paid bankers and stockbrokers who concentrate in the city of London. There are now some excellent restaurants run by British chefs serving new interpretations of traditional British dishes. It would, however, be a great mistake to assume that there has been any shift in eating habits in general. Bland, starchy foods reign supreme. Many British people do not eat at all, but just

味気ない食事が幅を利かせている。そもそも英国人の多くは食事というものをいっさいとらず、菓子やチョコレートやポテトチップなどのおやつしか食べないし、ほとんど液体食（ビール）のみで生存している者すらいるのである。

英国の食生活でただ1つ評価できるのは、中華料理、インド料理、そしてイタリア料理のレストランだろう。中華料理のレストランなどが出す料理は、日本のそれよりもおいしく、料金も安い。

食事に対する英国人の姿勢も、悲しいことに、階級意識と愛国心によって歪められている。英国人は、自国の食事はシンプルかもしれないが、少なくとも誠実で信頼できると考えている。それに対してフランス料理は、"料理名がめめしく" "ちゃらちゃらして" いて "お上品" である。おいしいものを食べることは、みずからの階級の価値観に対する背徳行為なのだ。

それでも英国は、おいしい料理を好む人々が住む善良な国家である。スーパーマーケットに行けば生鮮食品が日本よりはるかに安い値段で手に入るし、（英国のほとんどのものがそうであるように）地場産業との競争も輸入規制もないために、市場には輸入食品や輸入ワインがあふれている。気に入った食材を買ってきて自宅でご馳走をつくることもできれば、世界各国の料理を本場の味そのままに提供してくれるレストランに出かけることもできるのだ。

Q: 英国はほんとうに紅茶中毒者の国なのか？

紅茶は英国人の生活のなかできわめて重要な地位を占めている。なぜなら紅茶は、英国人にそのわずかな活力のすべてを供給している活力源だからだ。紅茶がなかったら、英国人は仕事をす

snack on sweets, chocolate, and potato chips; others contrive to exist off an almost entirely liquid diet (beer).

One positive feature of the British culinary scene are the Chinese, Indian, and Italian restaurants. The Chinese restaurants, by the way, are both better and cheaper than in Japan.

Tragically, class and national consciousness manage to warp the attitudes of British people toward what they eat! British food is regarded as simple, but at least honest and trustworthy. French food, by contrast, is "fancy" and "posh" with "poncey sounding names." To eat good food is to betray the values of one's own class.

Despite all this, the U.K. is a good country for people who like good food. Fresh food at the supermarket is far cheaper than in Japan, and (as with most things in Britain) the absence of any local competition or import restrictions means that the market is flooded with imported food and wine. You can buy whatever ingredients you need to cook splendid meals at home, or alternatively you can go out to restaurants serving good, authentic food from all over the world.

Q: Are the British really a nation of tea addicts?

Tea is a very important part of British life because it provides British people with all of the very little energy that they have. If there were no tea, British people would be quite unable to get out of bed, let alone work. More than North Sea Oil, it is

ることはおろか、朝ベッドから出ることもできない
だろう。英国の経済を動かしているほんとうの燃
料は、北海原油ではなく紅茶なのである。フラン
ス人はレモンやハーブを入れた繊細な味わいの
紅茶を飲むが、かならずミルクを入れる英国人は、
ケニアやアッサムなどの香りの強い濃い紅茶を好
む。

　紅茶を飲む英国人の習慣を、外国人はなにか
非常に上品なものと捉えているようである。キリ
ン・ビバレッジの"午後の紅茶"の缶には、午後5
時に紅茶を飲む習慣を始めたと伝えられるベッド
フォード第7代公爵夫人、アンナの肖像画が描かれ
ている。フォートナム・アンド・メイソンの高価な紅
茶や、ウェッジウッド、ロイヤル・ドルトンなどのティ
ーカップは格好のロンドンみやげだ。日本人は英
国人のアフタヌーンティの習慣を、きわめて様式化
された日本の茶の湯と関連づけて考えるせいか、
なおさらアフタヌーンティに貴族的なイメージを持
つようだ。この世にこれ以上の大きな誤解はある
まい。

　英国人はしょっちゅう紅茶を飲むから、これを厳
粛な儀式にするのは不可能である。紅茶は英国で
消費される飲料のじつに43パーセントを占めてい
る。毎日10人のうち8人の英国人が、少なくとも1杯
の紅茶を飲んでいる。紅茶を飲む習慣があまりに
も蔓延しているため、英国経済の衰退の原因はお
茶の時間に休憩するためではないかと言われてい
るほどである。なにかとてつもない悲劇が起きる
と、英国人は真心こもった慰めの言葉をかけ合う
代わりに、"濃くておいしい紅茶"を勧め合う。実
際、1940年代に英国全土にその名を轟かせた連続
殺人犯、ジョン・レジナルド・クリスティは、いまお
茶をいれているところだと言って被害者を安心さ
せておいてから殺害の手はずを整えた。

the real fuel driving the British economy. While the French drink subtle blends of tea flavored with lemon or herbs, the British, who always add milk, prefer cruder and stronger teas such as Kenya or Assam.

Among foreigners the British ritual of tea drinking is seen as something very genteel. Kirin Beverage's cans of "Afternoon Tea" feature a portrait of Anna, seventh Duchess of Bedford, who is said to have started the practice of drinking tea at 5 o'clock in the afternoon. Expensive cans of Fortnum and Mason teas or a set of Wedgwood or Royal Doulton teacups make excellent gifts or souvenirs from London. Tea's aristocratic image is only reinforced by the tendency of the Japanese to associate English afternoon tea with the highly formalized patterns of the tea ceremony in Japan. Nothing could be more wrong.

The British drink tea much too frequently to make a solemn ritual out of it. Consider these extraordinary statistics. Tea accounts for 43 percent of drinks consumed in Britain. Every day eight out of ten Britains have at least one cup of tea. Tea drinking is so rampant that the overfondness of the British working man for his tea break has even been proposed as an explanation for Britain's economic decline! At moments of extreme tragedy, British people console each other not with heartfelt advice but with the offer of "a nice strong cup of tea." Indeed, John Reginald Christie, a celebrated serial killer from the 1940s, always reassured his victims with the promise that he was making them a cup of tea, when in fact he was making preparations to kill them.

頻繁に紅茶を飲む英国人は、すさまじく機能的な飲み方をする。英国で飲まれる紅茶の約90パーセントがティーバッグの紅茶である。カップにも、上等な陶磁器ではなくマグカップが使われる。喫茶店で紅茶を頼めば、カップのなかでティーバッグが泳いでいることすらあるほどだ。これが今日の英国における、悲しくも浅ましいアフタヌーンティの実体である。優雅な伝統は、見苦しい利便性の前に放棄されたのである。

Q: 英国人はなぜあんなにたくさんチョコレートやキャンディを食べるのか？

英国人は食事に関してはじつに不真面目だが、おやつに関しては恐ろしいほど真剣である。チョコレートとキャンディとポテトチップの市場は、ポップミュージック、コメディ、そしてタクシーとともに、英国経済のなかでも活気が見られる数少ない業界の一つだ。

日本人は日に3度の食事を真面目にとろうとするが、そのための買い物や料理に要するまめさも時間管理の技術も、英国人には欠けている。そのために英国人は、いつまでたっても子どもっぽい食習慣から抜けだせず、肥満や吹き出物の原因になるものだけを食べつづけることになる。

キャンディ市場には、いくつかの大企業が君臨している。そのなかの1つ、ラウントリー・マッキントッシュ社はヨーク市を本拠とする製菓会社で、世界じゅうにキットカットとポロ・ミントを供給し、現在ではネッスル社の傘下に入っている。マース社は、"1日1本マースを食べてよく遊び、よく学ぼう"というキャッチフレーズで知られるマース・バーを世に送りだしているアメリカの企業である。キャドバリー・シュウェップス社は英国最大の製菓会

Tea is so popular in Britain that it is drunk in a brutally functional manner. Almost 90 percent of tea made in Britain is brewed from tea bags! The tea thus made is then drunk not from fine china, but from mugs. In certain cafés the tea is actually served with the teabag still floating around inside. This is the sad and sordid reality of tea drinking in Britain today. Elegant tradition has been rejected in favor of unsightly convenience.

Q: Why do the British eat so much chocolate and candy?

The British are not serious about food, but they are deadly serious about snacks. The market for chocolate, candy, and potato chips is—along with pop music, comedy, and taxi-driving—one of the few areas where any dynamism can be found in the U.K. economy.

While the Japanese are very serious about getting their three meals a day, the British lack the organization and time-management skills required either to shop or to cook. They consequently live in an eternal gastronomic childhood, eating only those things guaranteed to make them both fat and spotty.

The candy market is dominated by a few giant companies. Rowntree-Mackintosh is a York-based confectionery manufacturer which gave the world Kit-Kat and Polo mints, and is now a branch of Nestle; Mars, an American company, is the home of the Mars Bar with its slogan: "A Mars a day helps you work, rest and play." Cadbury Schweppes is the biggest British-owned confectionery company with an annual turnover of over £2 billion (US$3.2 billion), and has recently acquired the 7-Up and Dr. Pepper brands. And then there is the McVitie

社で、年間20億ポンド（32億ドル）の総収益をあげ
ており、先頃セブンアップとドクター・ペッパーの
ブランドを買収した。マクビティ・グループ（ユナイ
テッド・ビスケット社の1部門）は、ダイジェスティ
ブ・ビスケットで日本でもよく知られている。

　ほかにも、フィッシャーマンズ・フレンドという刺
激の強い茶色のメンソールキャンディを日本でも販
売しているロフトハウス社のような中小企業が数
多く存在する。

　お菓子は紅茶と同じく、本質的に不公平に出来
ていると英国人が考えるこの世界を生き抜くため
に、彼らがすがるささやかな慰めの1つである。

Q: パブはほんとうにそんなに人気があるのか？

　"およそ人間が考えだしたもののなかで、酒場や
宿屋ほど多くの幸せを生みだしたものはほかにな
い"と、18世紀の文学者サミュエル・ジョンソン博
士がいみじくも言ったように、今日にいたるまでパ
ブの人気は高く、英国の象徴の1つでありつづけ
ている。

　それでも近年、手強い競争相手が出現し、パブ
人気は急速に衰えはじめた。フランス風のカフェ
やしゃれたバーがパブの常連客を奪う一方で、エ
クスタシーのような麻薬（脱水症に陥らないために
ミネラルウォーターと一緒に飲む）の濫用が広が
り、ビールは若者にとってかつての魅力を失った。

　理想的なパブとは、日本の風呂屋のように近所
の人たちが分け隔てなく集まってくつろぎ、交流
を深められる場所である。だが最近は"パブのア
パルトヘイト"とも呼ぶべき現象が起き、ロンドン
の金融街"シティ"にあるパブのなかには、ピンス
トライプのスーツに身を固めた儲けすぎの若い証

Group (a branch of United Biscuits) that is well known in Japan for its Digestive biscuits.

There are also many smaller firms such as Lofthouse, which makes Fisherman's Friends, the extra strong brown-coloured mints which are distributed in Japan.

Confectionery is, like tea, one of the small consolations that help the British people soldier on in what they regard as a fundamentally unfair world.

Q: Are pubs really so popular?

The eighteenth century man of letters Dr. Samuel Johnson famously observed that, "There is nothing which has yet been contrived by man, by which so much happiness is produced as by a good tavern or inn," and to this day the pub remains a popular institution and one of the symbols of Britain.

Pubs have recently experienced a dramatic decline in popularity due to new competition. French-style cafés and designer bars have lured away many pub-goers, while the widespread use of recreational drugs such as Ecstasy (usually consumed with a bottle of mineral water to prevent dehydration) means that beer no longer has the appeal it once had for the young.

The ideal pub should be like a Japanese public bath, with all the people of the neighborhood meeting together in a relaxed, friendly way. Recently, however, a kind of "pub apartheid" has appeared, with pubs in the City, the business heart of London, denying entry to workmen in dirty work clothes so that the overpaid young stockbrokers and traders in

券マンやトレーダーが、劣った(すなわち低賃金の)人々の目を気にすることなく巨額のボーナスを心おきなく自慢しあえるようにとの配慮から、作業着を着た労働者の出入りを拒否する店が現れた。それでも幸いにして、"スーツお断り"のパブ(ノーパン喫茶とは無関係)が登場して反撃が始まっている。

市場の変化が起きる前から、パブはすでに深刻な問題に直面していた。国民に節制を促すために第1次世界大戦中に定められた開店時間は、不便なことこの上なかった。パブは昼食時に開店するが、午後になると店を閉め、夕方にまた店を開けて、午後11時には看板になってしまうのである。しかも、最近は英国人もさまざまな料理や飲み物に親しんで舌を肥やしているというのに、パブは相も変わらずビール、ウィスキー、ジュース、炭酸飲料などの飲み物と、ポテトチップやお決まりの料理しか出さず、嗜好の多様化に対応しようとしなかった。

そのパブもいまようやく眠りから覚め、戦いに挑みはじめている。生き残りをかけて変わりはじめたのである。

Q: ウィスキーの起源は?

"ウィスキー"という言葉はゲール語で"命の水"を意味する"ウィシュカ・ベーハ"に由来している。ウィスキーがアイルランドからスコットランドにもたらされたのは紀元400年ごろと言われているが、文字の形で記録に残っているものとしては1494年の文書がもっとも古い。蒸留酒は何世紀ものあいだ、スコットランド北部の小さな蒸留所で、多くの場合違法に、そして小規模に製造されていた。今日の私たちにも親しみのあるブランドのウィスキ

pin-stripe suits can bray loudly about their huge bonuses without having to see lesser (meaning less well-paid) beings. The good news is that a counterattack is under way with the introduction of the "no suit" pub (not related to the "*no-pan kisa*").

Pubs had serious problems even before the market dynamics changed. Their opening hours—introduced during World War I to encourage temperance—were extremely inconvenient. Opening for lunch, they closed again in the afternoon, then opened once more in the evening before closing once and for all at the early hour of 11 P.M. Pubs were also slow to diversify, content to offer beer, spirits, soft drinks, crisps, and unimaginative food when the public was developing a taste for more sophisticated and varied food and drink.

Pubs have now begun to shake off their apathy and are fighting back—adapting to survive!

Q: What are the origins of whisky?

The word "whisky" comes from the Gaelic *uisege beatha*, which means "water of life." Whisky is supposed to have been introduced to Scotland from Ireland around the year 400, but the first written record dates from 1494. Distilling was for many centuries a small-scale affair carried out in small and often illegal stills in the highlands. The commercially produced whiskey brands that we know today generally date from the late nineteenth century.

一の大半は、19世紀末になってから大量生産されるようになった。

19世紀末にウィスキーの人気が沸騰した理由については、これまで様々に説明されてきた。スコットランドの起業家たちに勢いがあったためであるとか、巨大な世界市場のほとんどに英国船が出入りしていたため、スコットランドとイングランドが鉄道でつながったため、スコットランド関係のものが流行した（サー・ウォルター・スコットの人気によって火がつき、ビクトリア女王のバルモラル城購入によって決定的になった）ため、などと言われている。

これら数々の要因のなかでもっとも重要なのは、不認可の蒸留所による醸造を厳しく罰するとともに輸出税を引き下げるという法改正がなされ、ウィスキーの大量生産が促されたことと、1860年代にフランスで葉枯れ病が蔓延し、ブドウ畑が荒廃したことである。フランスのブドウ畑が荒廃したことにより、当時英国でもっとも人気の高い蒸留酒だったブランデーが不足し、人々はブランデーのソーダ割りからウィスキーの水割りに鞍替えせざるを得なかった。今日の多くの人気ブランドの歴史はこのころ始まったものである。ホワイトマッカイは1882年に製造が開始され、グレンフィディックは1887年、ホワイトホースは1890年だった。

最近では高価なシングルモルト（単一の蒸留所でつくられたブレンドしないウィスキー）の売り上げが伸びる一方で、ブレンドウィスキーは宣伝販売に工夫を凝らしたその他の蒸留酒に地盤を奪われはじめている。ウィスキーはこれまで伝統を売りにしてきたが、結果的に古臭くて野暮な飲み物というイメージがつきまとうようになった。

Many explanations have been put forward for the dramatic surge in the popularity of whisky in the last decades of the nineteenth century. These include the dynamism of Scottish entrepreneurs, the existence of a huge global market served largely by British ships, the linking of Scotland and England by rail, and the fashion for things Scottish (set by Sir Walter Scott and sealed by Queen Victoria with her purchase of Balmoral).

Of these many factors the most significant are first, legislative changes which encouraged commercial whisky production by imposing stricter penalties for unlicensed distilling while lowering export duties; and second, the blight that ravaged French vineyards in the 1860s. This resulted in a shortage of brandy—which until that time had been the the most popular spirit in Britain—and many drinkers had no choice but to switch from brandy and soda to whisky and water. Many of the brands that are popular today originated at this time. For example, Whyte and Mackay dates from 1882, Glenfiddich from 1887, and White Horse from 1890.

In recent years the market has changed, with sales of expensive single malts (unblended whiskies coming from a single distillery) booming, while blends have begun to lose ground to other more imaginatively marketed spirits. Whisky has generally made tradition the base of its appeal, but the result is that it is now perceived as an old-fashioned, fuddy-duddy's drink.

娯楽・スポーツ

Q: 英国はなぜこれほど多くのスポーツを生んだのか？

　　ゴルフ、テニス、競馬、スカッシュ、サッカー、ラグビー、クリケット——驚くほど多くのスポーツが英国から生まれている。その理由は、英国の圧倒的な豊かさに求めることができるだろう。"バブル景気"に湧いた1980年代の日本に次々とゴルフコースが造られたことを見ても、国が豊かになればなるほど人が余暇に費やす金額も増えることは明らかである。

　　英国は、少なくとも18世紀にはほかのどの国家よりも豊かだったし、議会制民主主義のおかげで、その富はより広範囲に行き渡った。王室や貴族の後ろ盾を得て、18世紀末に競馬やボクシングなど賭けの対象となるスポーツが人気を博し、英国でもっとも有名な平場のレースであるダービーが1780年に始まった。

　　19世紀に入り、パブリックスクールが設立されると、スポーツはますます盛んになった。従来若者の遊びにすぎなかったものが、富裕な中流階級の子息の肉体と精神を養うために創設されたパブリックスクールにおいて、スポーツとしての形を整えた。ラグビーという名称も、ラグビーを考案したパブリックスクールの校名に由来しているし、サッカー協会の設立にもパブリックスクールは大きな役割を果たした。

　　19世紀後半から20世紀初頭にかけて人々が郊外へ移り住むようになると、芝生を利用したスポーツが盛んになり、1873年にウェールズでテニスが考案され、2度の世界大戦の合間にゴルフの人気が高まった。

Q: Why did so many sports originate in Britain?

Golf, tennis, horse-racing, squash, football, rugby, cricket—an extraordinary number of sports originated in Britain. The reason for this lies in Britain's extraordinary prosperity. The great number of golf courses built in Japan during the years of the 1980s "bubble economy" show that, even now, the more prosperous a country is, the greater the sums people spend on leisure.

Britain, at least from the eighteenth century, was richer than any other country, and, thanks to Parliamentary democracy those riches were spread more widely. Under the patronage of royalty and the aristocracy, sports such as horse-racing and boxing, both popular for betting, flourished in the late years of that century, with the Derby, Britain's most famous horse-race, dating from 1780.

Sports received a further boost with the founding of the public schools in the early nineteenth century. In these institutions, established as much to cultivate the bodies as the minds of the sons of the prosperous middle-classes, traditional street sports were formalized. Rugby actually derives its name from the English public school where it was invented, while public schools were also instrumental in setting up the Football Association.

In the late nineteenth and early twentieth centuries the growth of the suburbs was accompanied by a surge in lawn sports such as tennis, which was invented in Wales in 1873, and golf, which became popular between the two World Wars.

Q: サッカーが絶大な人気を誇る背景は？

英国は数々のスポーツを生んだが、そのなかでも英国人がフットボールと呼ぶサッカーの人気に勝るものはないだろう。"ビューティフル・スポーツ"という愛称で呼ばれるサッカーこそ、まさに英国のスポーツである。

そもそもサッカーは、ロンドンの街中で見習い工たちが興じる乱暴な球技にすぎなかったが、19世紀半ばに入ってパブリックスクールの授業にとり入れられるようになるとルールが整えられ、FAカップが出現した1870年代ごろには、労働者階級の文化に欠くことのできないスポーツになっていた。

海外に工場を設立した英国人技師らによって、サッカーは他国でもその地位を確立した。サッカーが世界じゅうで愛されているのはこのためである。英国はみずからが発明したスポーツ競技においてほかの国にお株を奪われることで有名だが、サッカーもまた例外ではない。ワールドカップの成績を見ても、ブラジルは4度も優勝し、イタリアと西ドイツも3度優勝を飾っているにもかかわらず、英国は1966年にたった1度優勝したのみである。

英国人選手がヨーロッパ大陸や南米の選手ほどのテクニックを持たないのは事実かもしれないが、それでも英国リーグは海外でも高く評価されている。プレミアリーグに君臨するリバプール、マンチェスター・ユナイテッド、アーセナルなどの強豪チームは、FAカップやリーグ・チャンピオンシップで競い合うのみならず、ヨーロピアン・カップのようなヨーロッパのトーナメントの常連にもなっている。

暴力行為と劣悪なグランドのおかげで、1980年代までサッカーのイメージは芳しくなかったが、最近はサッカー界も商売を意識するようになった。

Q: **What is the background to football's enormous popularity?**

Of the many sports that originated in Britain,
none can match the huge popularity of soccer
(called football in the U.K.). Nicknamed "the
beautiful game," it is the British national sport
par excellence.

Football originated as a violent game played
by apprentices in the streets of London, acquired
rules through being played at public schools in the mid-nine-
teenth century, and, by the 1870s, with the advent of the FA
(Football Association) Cup, had become an integral part of
working-class culture.

The game was established in other countries by British
engineers who went to set up factories abroad. Hence its international popularity. Britain is famous for losing to other countries in the sports it invented, and football is no exception.
Britain has won the World Cup only once, in 1966, as opposed
to Brazil's four wins, or Italy and West Germany's three wins.

The British may lack some of the finesse of European or
Latin-American players, but its league is internationally
respected. The leading teams in the Premier League such as
Liverpool, Manchester United, and Arsenal, as well as contest-
ing the FA Cup and the League Championship, regularly par-
ticipate in European championships such as the European Cup.

Up till the 1980s, the game suffered from an image problem with violence and run-down grounds, but it has recently
become much more commercially savvy. Clubs have been

サッカークラブの中には株式を上場したり、テレビ局と独占放送の交渉をしたり、巧みに物品を販売したりして、資金を稼ぎはじめているところもある。英国チームに所属できる外国人選手の人数制限は撤廃され、世界でもトップレベルの選手たちが英国のリーグで腕を競い合うようになった。デイビッド・ベッカムのようなスター選手はポップスター並みの扱いを受け、巨額の年俸を支給され、商品宣伝にひと役買って大金を稼ぎ、スパイスガールと結婚までしている。

Q: サッカー・フーリガンとは実際のところなんなのか？

サッカーは19世紀の労働者階級の文化に深く根ざしたスポーツである。サッカーと言えば昔から、労働者が"メイト（友だち）"と連れだって地元チームを応援に出かけるものと決まっていた。したがって、サッカーの観客の大半は男である。ほとんどのスタジアムには、つい最近まで座席ではなくひな壇型の立ち見席が用意されていた。ファンはそれぞれ場所を陣取って歌を唄うが、それは晶員（ひいき）チームを応援するためというよりは、むしろ相手チームに対して敵意をむきだしにするためである。大量のアルコールが試合の前後に消費され、酔っぱらって興奮し大声を張りあげる男たちが醸しだす独特の雰囲気は、新聞各紙上で"部族闘争"と表現されてきた。

このような一触即発の雰囲気に乗じて暴力行為を働くのがフーリガンである。彼らはダーツや重い1ポンド硬貨、スタンレーナイフなどを武器に使う。英国のフーリガンは1990年と1998年のワールドカップでも海外のマスコミの注目を浴びたが、もっとも名高い"実績"は、ブリュッセルのヘイゼルで開催され、死者38人（うち37名がイタリア人）を

raising money by floating themselves on the stock exchange, by negotiating exclusive deals with TV stations, and by skillful merchandizing. Regulations restricting the number of foreign players who can play in a British team have been scrapped, and the British game features many of the world's top talents. Soccer stars like David Beckham live like pop idols, receiving colossal salaries, making big money from product endorsements, and even marrying Spice Girls!

Q: What exactly are football hooligans?

Soccer has deep roots in nineteenth century working-class culture. Traditionally working men went to support their local team with their "mates" (friends). Thus, it is a sport watched by a largely male audience. Until recently most stadiums featured not seats but terraces, where fans stood to watch games. The fans are divided into different areas and sing songs often not so much in support of their team as hostile to their opponents. Large quantities of alcohol are consumed before and after the game, and the atmosphere created by this concentration of drunk, over-excited chanting males is often described in the newspapers as "tribal."

Hooligans take advantage of this already tense and aggressive atmosphere to indulge in acts of violence. Their weapons include darts, heavy one-pound coins, and Stanley knives. While British hooligans have been the focus of international press attention at both the 1990 and 1998 World Cups, their most notorious "achievement" was at the 1985 European Cup Final between Liverpool and Juventus at Heysel in Brussels, in

出した1985年のヨーロッパカップ決勝戦、リバプール対ユベントス戦である。

サッカー界のスポークスマンによると、暴力行為に走るのはごく少数で、その少数派のために英国の一般的なサッカーファンのイメージが台無しにされているという。実際、調査の結果、相手チームのサポーターと一戦交えることだけを目的にして特定チームを応援するチンピラ集団の存在が明らかになった。そのなかでもとくに有名なのは、インターシティ・ファーム（ウェスト・ハム）とサービス・クルー（リーズ・ユナイテッド）である。彼ら"プロのフーリガン"の多くが、平日にはちゃんとした仕事についているというのだから驚きである。

Q: なぜ英国にはフーリガンが多いのか？

上品な紳士の住む国と思われている英国がフーリガンの多さで世界一だとは、いったいどういうわけだろうか？　なにが人をフーリガンへと駆りたてるのだろう？

サッカー・フーリガンは英国に限った現象でないことを、まず心に留めておく必要があるだろう。ドイツやオランダにも暴力的なファンは存在する。風土による国民性の違いが大きな要因になっているのかもしれない。南ヨーロッパの男たちは、女性を誘惑することによってみずからの男らしさを確認する。これに対して南ヨーロッパの男たちに比べて容姿が劣り、魅力に欠ける北ヨーロッパの男たちは、男同士で戦うことによってしか男らしさを表現できない。南ヨーロッパの男は優しさを示すことによって女性に認めてもらおうとするが、北ヨーロッパの男は暴力に訴えることによってほかの男たちに認めてもらおうとするのである。

もう1つの眉唾ものの説明は、悲惨な世界大戦

which thirty-eight people (thirty-seven of them Italians) were crushed to death.

Spokesmen from the world of soccer insist that hooliganism is the work of a minority group whose bad behavior is wrecking the image of British fans generally. Investigations have indeed revealed that there are gangs associated with the major clubs whose sole purpose is to fight with the supporters of other teams. Of these the InterCity Firm (West Ham) and the Service Crew (Leeds United) were the most notorious. It is a surprising fact that many of these "professional hooligans" have respectable jobs in the weekdays.

Q: Why does Britain have so many hooligans?

Why does a country whose stereotype would have us believe is inhabited only by gentlemen with exquisite manners lead the world in hooliganism? What motivates people to become hooligans?

First of all, it is important to note that football hooliganism is not an exclusively British phenomenon. Germany and Holland also have violent fans. Regional character may be an important factor. Southern European males assert their maleness by seducing women. Northern European men, by contrast, are much more ugly and much less charming and can only express their maleness by brutish male-on-male violence. While the Southern European man seeks to win the approval of women through gentleness, the Northern European man seeks to win the approval of his male peers through violence.

Another rather dubious theory of hooliganism proposes

の記憶が薄らいだことによって、暴力への集団的な希求が高まったというものである。つまり、第2次世界大戦の記憶が生々しかった1955年には、英国のサッカーファンは"教会で礼拝する信徒のように秩序ある"行動をとっていたというのだ。戦争の恐怖を体験していない世代は、暴力は快感だという誤った思い込みを持っているというのである。

わたしの理論はこうだ。内気で社交下手の英国人にとって、攻撃性は内気さの裏返しにすぎないのである。結局のところ、いったん誰かを殴ってしまえば、その人と前向きにつき合っていく必要はなくなるのだから。暴力をふるってしまえば、みずからの社交下手に気づかずにすむのである。1998年のワールドカップ開催中に、電車のなかで微笑みかけてきたフランス人を刺したイギリス人サッカーファンの事件は、私のこの理論を見事に裏づけている。そのイギリス人フーリガンは、彼自身よりわずかでも前向きで友好的で、彼ほど破壊的でも愚かでもない行動をとる人間と向き合ったとき、どう対応すればいいのかわからなかったのである。

Q: 英国人はなぜあんなに賭事が好きなのか？

英国人は賭事が大好きである。街のメインストリートにはかならず賭博場が店を開いている。新聞店に入れば、その場で現金があたるスクラッチカードを買うことができる。土曜の夜にテレビをつければ、国営宝くじの抽選生放送を観ることができる。

賭事はどこの国でも大人気で、日本でもパチンコ業界の年間総売り上げはおもな自動車会社のそれを上まわっているが、昔からスポーツの盛んな英国ではとりわけ人気が高い。賭博場は外から見

that as memories of the horrors of war subside, the collective urge to violence increases. Thus, in 1955, when memories of World War II were still fresh, a British soccer crowd was said to be as "orderly as a church meeting". Later generations who have not experienced the horrors of war mistakenly think that violence is fun.

I have my own theory. For British people who are terribly socially awkward, aggression is no more than the flip side of shyness. After all, if you hit someone, you are released from having to relate to them in any constructive way. Violence helps you to avoid having to face your own social inadequacies. A story that an English fan stabbed a Frenchman who smiled at him on the train during the 1998 World Cup sums up my point perfectly. The hooligan was unable to deal with anything positive, anything friendly, anything less destructive and mindless than himself.

Q: Why are the British crazy about gambling?

The British love gambling. Walk down any high street and you will always find a betting shop. Go into any newsagent's and you can buy scratch cards that offer instant cash prizes. Switch on the television on a Saturday night, and you can watch the National Lottery draw live.

Betting is popular all over the world—in Japan the annual turnover of the pachinko business is higher than that of its leading car manufacturing sector—but in Britain, because the country has a very long sporting tradition, it is particularly so.

えないように窓に目隠しがされ、床は安っぽいリ
ノリューム張りで、むさ苦しくみすぼらしい雰囲気
を漂わせているが（見栄えのいい店をつくること
を法律で禁じられている）、たいていの場合、一
流の会計士が運営する巨大国際コングロマリット
の一部である。

　スポーツのなかで賭けの対象としてもっとも一
般的なのは、サッカー賭博を通して賭けるサッカ
ーと、競馬である。ただし英国人は、どんなもの
にでも賭ける心構えが常に整っており、賭博場の
チェーン店では、半年以内にエルヴィス・プレスリ
ーが生き返る確率や、スキャンダルに揺れるクリ
ントン大統領がいつまでホワイトハウスに留まれる
かといった賭けが行われている。“ブッキー”と呼
ばれる賭けの胴元が出すオッズは世論をきわめて
正確に反映していることから、総選挙の時期にな
るとニュースでたびたびとり上げられるほどであ
る。

　ギャンブル人気に火がついたのは、国営宝くじ
が始まった1994年11月のことだった。いまでは成
人男女の3分の2が宝くじを買っており、開始から
の3年間で100万ポンドを超える当たりが460本も
出た。1994年に英国人がギャンブルに費やした費
用は合計で37億ポンドだったが、1995年には53億
ポンドに跳ね上がり、昔ながらの賭事（宝くじと違
って宣伝を禁じられている）は危機感をおぼえて
いる。

　製造業が国際的な地位を奪われながらも、不誠
実な証券ブローカーや不動産開発業者のおかげ
でなんとか1980年代を乗り切った英国経済は“カ
ジノ経済”と揶揄されることが多かった。国営宝く
じの創設によって、英国は文字通りカジノ国家に
なったと言えそうだ。

Although betting shops with their blanked-out windows and linoleum floors often look squalid and shabby (by law they are forbidden to be attractive places), they are frequently subsidiaries of large multinational conglomerates run by respectable accountants.

The sports most commonly bet on are football, through the football (as soccer is called in Britain) pools, and horse-racing. The British, however, are prepared to bet on anything, and the big betting chains will give you odds on the chances of Elvis Presley turning up alive in the next six months, or how long a scandal-rocked President Clinton is likely to stay in office. At the time of Britain's general elections, the odds given by the "bookies" (book-makers) are often reported on the news, since they serve as a very accurate indicator of public opinion.

The culmination of this gambling fever came in November 1994, when the National Lottery was launched. Played by two-thirds of the entire adult population, the lottery had payed out 460 wins of over £1 million each within three years of its establishment. Gambling expenditure jumped from £3.7 billion in 1994 to £5.3 billion in 1995, and traditional forms of betting (which unlike the lottery were forbidden to advertise) were feeling the pinch.

Britain, in the 1980s, divested of manufacturing industry but crawling with spivvy stockbrokers and property developers, was often called a "casino economy." The establishment of the National Lottery made it quite literally so!

Q: 英国人はなぜ休暇をとるのが好きなのか？

　現代の英国人が国家の衰退に無関心なのは、英国人が「歴史から休暇をもらっているからだ」と、ある著名な歴史家は指摘している。数百年間にわたって先頭を突っ走ってきた英国人は、帝国時代から溜め込んだ疲労をいまも引きずっており、当分はひたすらぼんやり時間を過ごしたいと願っている。

　英国人は休暇をとるのが大好きである。実際、バケーションの計画を立てるのと同じくらい大胆かつ熱心に仕事をしていれば、英国経済はこれほどひどい状況におちいらずにすんだはずだと思われるほどだ。

　1950年代までは、海外で休暇を過ごすことができるのは裕福な人たちに限られていた。当時金持ちがニースやカンヌやフィレンツェに群がっているあいだ、それほど裕福でない人たちはブライトンやボーンマスなどの英国内の海沿いの町で満足しなければならなかった。英国のリゾート地にも海沿いの遊歩道や桟橋や浜辺はあるが、そこには肝心な要素が欠けていた。すなわち、太陽である。

　1950年代以降は国家全体が豊かになり、どんな階級の英国人でも海外で休暇を過ごすことができるようになった。行き先としてはスペインが長らく一番人気だった（1996年に海外旅行をした英国人の4分の1がスペインへ行った）が、ユーロトンネルの開通によって最近はフランスが人気を集めはじめている。

　スペインもフランスも結構な国ではあるが、この両国には2つの重大な欠点がある。まず第1に、地元民が英語を話せない。そして第2に、食事がうんざりするほど洗練されている。このため、低俗であること間違いなしのアメリカ合衆国の人気が高まっている。国民が英語を話し、ハンバーガー

Q: Why do the British love taking holidays?

A celebrated historian commenting on the indifference of modern-day British people to their country's decline suggested that they were enjoying a "holiday from history." After centuries of setting the pace, post-imperial fatigue had set in, and the common desire was to do nothing more than just vegetate contentedly.

On a literal level, too, the British love taking holidays. In fact, one suspects that if they were half as adventurous and painstaking about their jobs as they are about planning their vacations, the country might be in a better economic shape.

Until the 1950s, it was only the wealthy who could afford to take their holidays abroad. So while the rich flocked to Nice, Cannes, and Florence, the less well-off had to content themselves with a visit to an English seaside town, such as Brighton or Bournemouth. Although the British resorts had promenades, piers, and beaches, they lacked one crucial ingredient—the sun.

Since the late 1950s, increasing prosperity has enabled British people of all classes to take holidays abroad. Spain has long been the most popular destination (receiving over one-quarter of all British travelers in 1996), but since the opening of the Channel Tunnel, France is gaining ground.

Fine countries though these are, they do have two serious defects. First, the natives cannot speak English. Second, the food is tiresomely sophisticated. For this reason the reassuringly vulgar United States has become an increasingly popular destination. It is a home-away-from-home, where English-speaking hosts proffer burgers and chips.

とフライドポテトを食べさせてくれるアメリカは、英国人にとって第2の我が家のようなものなのだ。

近年の不況のあおりを受けて、ある日本の半導体メーカーが英国工場を閉鎖し、従業員を全員解雇するという出来事があった。このことは日本のマスコミでも詳しく報道され、職を失った元従業員の生の声も伝えられた。驚くべきことに、英国の従業員がもっとも心配したのは、失業することではなく、海外での休暇の予定をとりやめにしたりスケジュールを変更したりしなければならないことだった。

Q: 英国はほんとうに園芸家の国か？

日本人は職場でせっせと働いているときが一番幸せかもしれないが、英国人がもっとも幸せを感じるのは庭でのんびりしているときである。英国ではガーデニングの人気がきわめて高い。英国統計局の1998年の調査によると、男性の52パーセント、女性の45パーセントが定期的に庭の手入れをしているという。

温暖で湿度の高い英国の気候は（人を陰鬱な気分にさせるが）、植物の生育に適している。いわゆる"イングリッシュ・ガーデン"は、自然の成りゆきにまかせる庭づくりであり、まっすぐな砂利道と刈り込まれた生け垣からなるフランスの庭園が人の手で自然をコントロールしようとする試みそのものであるのとは対照的だ。

日本人は機械やテクノロジーを無条件で愛するが、英国人は現代の産業化社会に対してかねてより複雑な感情を抱いてきた。英国は世界で最初に産業革命を体験したために、ほかの国々よりはるかにすさまじい悪影響を被った。ひと握りの紡績工場経営者が巨万の富を築く一方で、自宅で糸を紡いだり機を織ったりしていた多くの人々が仕事

In the current economic downturn, a Japanese chip-maker closed its factory in the U.K., making all the staff redundant. This was extensively reported in the Japanese press, including comments from those who had lost their jobs. Extraordinarily, the most common complaint made by the British staff was not about the horror of unemployment, but about the tragedy of having to cancel or reschedule foreign holidays!

Q: Are the British really a nation of gardeners?

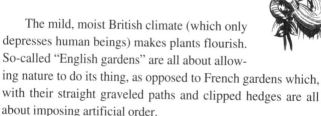

The Japanese may be happiest when toiling in an office, but the British are happiest when relaxing in a garden. Gardening is extremely popular in Britain. According to a 1998 survey by the Office of National Statistics, 52 percent of males and 45 percent of females gardened regularly.

The mild, moist British climate (which only depresses human beings) makes plants flourish. So-called "English gardens" are all about allowing nature to do its thing, as opposed to French gardens which, with their straight graveled paths and clipped hedges are all about imposing artificial order.

The Japanese love machines and technology unreservedly, but the British have always felt deeply ambivalent toward modern industrialized society. The Industrial Revolution happened first in Britain, and its short-term effects were therefore more violent, shocking, and entirely negative than anywhere else. A few spinning factory owners made huge fortunes, but masses of weavers and spinners who had been working in their

を失った。職を失った人々は煤で真っ黒に汚れた街へ移り住み、わずかな賃金のために劣悪な環境のもとで長時間働くことを余儀なくされた。

つまり英国でガーデニングの人気が高いのは、都会を逃れて、単純でより自然と調和のとれた産業革命以前の牧歌的な暮らしに戻りたいという国民の願望の表れなのである。

また、自立心が旺盛な英国人は、自分が食べる野菜をみずから育てることから得られる素朴な自給自足感覚を好む。さらにまた、"英国人の家はその城"という表現にも見られるとおり、自分の陣地を確保したいという欲求も関係しているのだ。

そもそも庭園は王室や貴族のものだった。16世紀に建てられたハンプトン・コート宮殿では、生け垣でつくられた見事な迷路を見ることができる。18世紀に入ると、豊かな貴族たちはケイパビリティ・ブラウンのような著名な園芸家を雇い入れ、クロード・ロランやニコラ・プーサンの絵画を彷彿させる庭園を設計させた。19世紀末になると、園芸の世界でも民主化が起こり、労働者が割当て地（地方自治体が市民に貸与する小区画の耕作地）で自家用野菜を育てはじめる一方で、中流階級の人々は郊外の"田園都市"へ移り住んだ。

世界の国々が豊かになり、英国人がとうの昔から知っていたこと——すなわち、一生懸命働くのはそれほどいいことではない——に気づきはじめたために、英国のガーデニング産業は輸出景気に湧いている。

Q: クリケットはどこがおもしろいのか？

クリケットは、インド、パキスタン、スリランカ、西インド連邦、オーストラリアなどの英連邦諸国で親しまれている。しかし、サッカー、テニス、ゴルフ

own cottages were thrown out of work and forced to move to squalid, coal-blackened towns, where they worked long hours in poor conditions for terrible wages.

The British love of gardens thus expresses a collective yearning to escape from the city back to a simpler, more natural, and more harmonious life, a pre-industrial rural idyll.

The British are also very independent people, and like the feeling of basic self-sufficiency gained from providing one's own vegetables with one's own hands. There is also an element of territorialism, of "an Englishman's home is his castle."

Originally gardens were the preserve of royalty and the aristocracy. Hampton Court, a sixteenth-century palace, includes a splendid hedge maze. In the eighteenth century, wealthy aristocrats would have their parks landscaped by celebrity gardeners such as Capability Brown to make them look like the paintings of Claude Lorrain or Nicolas Poussin. In the late nineteenth century, the democratization of gardens began, with workers growing their own vegetables in allotments (small plots of land rented from the local authorities), and the middle-classes moving out to "garden cities" in the suburbs.

As the world gets richer and realizes what the British have known for a long time, i.e., that working too hard is not such a good idea, the British gardening business is enjoying an export boom.

Q: What is the attraction of cricket?

Cricket is played in the countries of the British Commonwealth, such as India, Pakistan Sri Lanka, the West Indies, and Australia. Compared, however, to other British sports such as

などの英国生まれのその他のスポーツほど国際的人気を博すことはなかった。クリケットは英国独特のスポーツと見なされている。クリケット・ファンの目から見れば、これはつまり、クリケットは繊細なテクニックとフェアプレイ精神を誇る歴史あるスポーツだということになる。そしてクリケットが嫌いな人の目から見れば、退屈でお上品ぶった意味不明のスポーツということになるのだ。

外国人はクリケットと野球を混同していることが多いが、クリケットと野球はまったく別のスポーツである。クリケットは11名の選手からなる2つのチームで争われ、一方のチームが"攻撃側"のとき、もう一方は"守備側"となる。ピッチにはつねにふたりの打者がいるが、投手がワンバウンドで投げるボールのほうを向いているのはそのうち一方だけである。打者がボールを打つと、その打者はピッチの反対側に走り、反対側にいる打者も同様に走る。打者が1度（ピッチを）走るごとに1点が入る。投手の投げたボールが打者の背後にあるウィケットに当たった場合と、打ったボールがノーバウンドで守備側に捕られた場合は、打者（と打者のパートナー）はアウトとなる。

今よりはるかにのんびりしていた時代から伝わるクリケットの試合は数日間にもおよぶことがあるが、最近はテレビ中継の視聴率を上げるために1日で決着のつく短い試合が一般的になりつつある。クリケットはサッカーとは対照的に、暴力とは無縁のスポーツである。サイダーをしこたま飲んで日差しのなかに長時間座りつづけていたウェスト・カントリーのクリケットチームのサポーターが、座席のクッションを投げ合うことがあるくらいなものだ。なかには全裸になってピッチを走りまわって試合を活気づけようとするサポーターもおり、これは"ストリーキング"と呼ばれている。

soccer, tennis, or golf, it has failed to take root internationally. Cricket is regarded as the quintessentially English game. From a cricket-lover's point of view, this means it is a sport boasting a proud history, with an emphasis on subtle skills and fair play. From a cricket-hater's point of view, it means that it is unintelligible, boring, and infested with snobbery.

The majority of foreigners tend to confuse cricket with baseball. This is a mistake. In cricket there are two teams of eleven players. One team "bats" while the other team "fields." There are always two batsmen on the pitch, though only one of them faces the ball that is bowled at him by the bowler. If the batsman hits the ball he runs to the opposite end of the pitch, and the batsman opposite him does the same. One "run" (length of the pitch) is one point. The batsman is out if the bowled ball hits the wicket behind him, if he hits the ball and it is caught, or if he (or his partner) is run out.

Cricket matches—which herald from a more leisurely age—can go on for several days, though recently, to boost television audiences, shorter one-day matches are becoming more common. In comparison with soccer, cricket is a trouble-free sport. Supporters of West Country teams who have drunk too much cider and sat too long in the sun occasionally throw their seating cushions at one another. Other supporters feel inspired to liven up the game by taking off all their clothes and running across the pitch naked. This is called "streaking."

クリケットから生まれた慣用句は数多く、なかでも"フェアじゃない""ずるい"を意味する"クリケットじゃない"という表現はもっともよく使われている。

Q: ゴルフの起源は？

ゴルフは1300年ごろにオランダ人によって発明され、"コルフ"と呼ばれていたとする説がある。それでも、ゴルフに本当に熱心だったのはスコットランド人であり、国民がゴルフに熱中しすぎたために、ジェイムズⅡ世は1457年にゴルフを禁止したほどだった。ジェイムズⅥ世スコットランド王は1603年にジェイムズⅠ世イングランド王に即位し、ロンドン南部のブラックヒースに英国最初のゴルフコースを造った。

1754年に設立され、1834年にロイヤルの称号を冠せられたロイヤル・アンド・エンシェント・クラブ・オブ・セントアンドリュースは、アメリカを除く全世界においてゴルフルールの裁定機関として認められている。蛇にボールを呑み込まれたタイのプレーヤーや、聖牛にボールの上に座られたインドのプレーヤーの疑問に答えてルールを解釈するために、セントアンドリュースには1日24時間職員が詰めている。

昔はほとんどのゴルフコースがスコットランドの東海岸に造られたことから、シーサイドコース（海岸に面した砂丘に造られている）は古典的なゴルフコースとされ、全英オープンはつねにシーサイドコースで開催されてきた。

セントアンドリュース、ミュアフィールド、バークデール、サンドウィッチといったシーサイドコースは、全英オープンのおかげで世界的に有名である。一方で英国には、ウェントワース、サニングデ

Cricket has furnished the English language with a number of idioms of which the most commonly heard is the expression "It's just not cricket," meaning "it's unfair" or "someone is cheating."

Q: What are the origins of golf?

Some people claim that the Dutch invented the game around 1300 and called it *kolf* or *colf*. But it was the Scots who were so passionate about golf that in 1457 King James II passed an act forbidding it. James VI of Scotland, who became James 1 of England in 1603, had the first course in England built at Blackheath, to the south of London.

The Royal and Ancient Club of St. Andrews, founded in 1754 and formally instituted in 1834, is—except in the United States—accepted as the ruling body of the game. It has a member of staff on twenty-four-hour phone alert, ready to interpret the rules of the game to bemused players whose ball has been swallowed by a snake in Thailand or sat on by a sacred cow in India.

Since most of the early courses were established in the east coast of Scotland, links courses (courses built on sanddunes by the sea) became the classic course, and the British Open Championship is always held at such a course.

Links courses like St. Andrews, Muirfield, Birkdale, and Sandwich are known internationally because of the Open. There are, however, excellent inland courses such as Wentworth, Sunningdale, and Gleneagles. At famous courses it is

ール、グレンイーグルスなどの優れたインランドコ
ースも存在する。有名なコースではビジターがス
タート時間を確保するのはむずかしく、紹介状と
ハンディキャップ証明書が必要になる場合も多い。

　英国のゴルフの最大の長所は、上品ぶっていな
いことだろう。ほかの多くの国では（会員権に法外
な料金を支払わねばならない日本もその1つ）、ゴ
ルフは成金が競って金を使いたがる格好の見栄
消費の対象となっているが、英国ではゴルフには
ほとんど金がかからない。市営のコースなら1ラウ
ンドわずか5ポンドでまわれるし、セントアンドリュ
ースのような有名コースでも20ポンド以下である。
クラブの会員権もそれほど高くはないが、ただし
手続きは恐ろしく複雑で、順番待ちの列は気が遠
くなるほど長い。セントアンドリュース・クラブの
会員になるには、現在のところ18年間待たねばな
らないという。

often difficult for visitors to get a starting time, and a letter of introduction and a confirmation of handicap are often necessary.

The best feature of golf in Britain is its lack of snobbery. Whereas in many other countries (Japan, with its extortionate membership fees being one), golf is the *nouveaux riches*' favorite form of conspicuous consumption, British golf is extremely cheap. Municipal courses can cost as little as £5 for a round, while even famous courses like those at St. Andrews only cost between £23 and £75. Club membership is also not expensive, but the procedures are Byzantine and waiting lists are extremely long. The Royal and Ancient Club currently has a waiting list of eighteen years!

政治と王室

POLITICS & ROYALTY

Q: 英国議会の仕組みは？

　　国会は英国の最高立法府で、君主、上院、下院の3つから成り立っている。法案はこれらすべてを通過してはじめて成立する。

　　君主の役割は、実際のところは名目上のものにすぎない。君主は議会の開始を宣言し、上院と下院を通過した法案に署名するだけである。

　　上院は聖職上院議員（英国国教会の大主教と主教）と法官貴族（判事）、そして貴族上院議員で構成されている。貴族上院議員は上院の過半数を占めており、760人が世襲貴族で、380人が生涯貴族である。選挙で選ばれたわけでもない、爵位を持っているというだけの金持ちの集まりである上院は、しょっちゅう批判を浴びている。それでも、まったく同じ理由に基づいて上院を擁護する人々もいる。選挙で選ばれたわけではないからこそ、上院議員は政党の圧力と無関係に純粋に国益のみを考えて行動できるというわけだ。上院の役割は、下院を通過した法案を検討することである。

　　本当の意味で政治の場となっているのは下院である。下院は659人の国会議員からなり、その大半が男性議員で占められている。政権党は（安定半数を確保していれば）どんな法案でも思いのままに成立させることができる。

　　選挙は少なくとも5年に1度は実施される。659の選挙区で投票が行われ、もっとも多くの票を獲得した候補が議席を得る。"多数票主義"と呼ばれるこの制度は、総得票数に応じて各政党に議席が割り当てられる比例代表制に比べて非民主的で

Q: How does Britain's parliamentary system work?

Parliament is the highest legislative author-
ity in Britain. It consists of three parts: the
Monarch, the House of Lords, and the House
of Commons. Bills have to be passed by
all three parts before they can become law.

The Monarch's role is largely ceremonial and decorative. He or she officiates at
the opening of Parliament, and appends his or her signature to
bills that have already passed through the Commons and the
Lords.

The House of Lords is made up of the Lords Spiritual (the
archbishops and bishops of the Church of England), the Law
Lords (judges), and the Lords Temporal. This last group
makes up the majority of the house, with 760 hereditary peers
and 380 life peers. The House of Lords is frequently attacked
because it is an unelected assembly of titled rich people. Other
people defend it on precisely the same grounds, saying that the
Lords can do what is best for the country free from the pres-
sures of party politics. The Lords' function is to review legislation that has passed through the Commons.

The House of Commons is where the real action takes
place. It consists of 659 MPs (Members of Parliament) who
are mostly men. The party in power (provided it has a sufficent
majority) can put through any legislation it pleases.

Elections are held at least every five years. Votes are cast
in the 659 constituencies, and whatever party secures a majority wins the seat. This is called the "first past the post" system.
It is often attacked by the smaller parties (e.g., Liberal Democ-
rats) as undemocratic and unrepresentative compared to the

民意を反映しないとして、(自由民主党のような)
少数党からの批判にさらされている。

　英国議会は他の国々の民主政治のモデルにな
ったことから、"議会政治の母"とも呼ばれている。
議事堂は1000にのぼる部屋と100ヵ所の階段、3キ
ロメートルにおよぶ廊下を有するネオゴシック様式
の荘厳な建物で、一般公開されており、傍聴席か
ら審議を眺めることもできる。質疑応答の時間は、
ロンドン動物園のチンパンジーのお茶会に負けな
いくらいのおもしろさだ。

Q: 労働党と保守党の違いは？

　英国の政治体制は、基本的には労働党と保守
党が争う2大政党制である。保守党は金持ちと、
金持ちになろうとしている人々のための党であり、
一方の労働党は、貧しい人や、貧しい人の力にな
ろうとしている人々の党とされてきた。
　労働党は1900年の創設である。労働組合から
の資金によって運営され、党の使命は一般労働者
の権利を守るために戦うことだった。1945年の総
選挙で圧勝し、石炭や鉄道から航空会社にいた
るさまざまな産業を国営化して現代的な福祉国家
をつくりあげてはじめて、労働党はその実力を認
められた。労働党は富の再分配を重視している
が、富の創造には無頓着であり、(英国が世界一豊
かだった)エドワード王朝期には労働党の方針も
実現可能だったかもしれないが、分配されるべき
富の存在しない現代では現実味を失っている。
　保守党は昔から産業界の代弁者だった。"国家
は1つ"という考えを持つ古いタイプの保守党議員
は、憐憫の情と社会的責任にかられて資本主義の

proportional representation system, under which seats in Parliaments are distributed to political parties accor to their share of the overall vote.

The British Parliament is often called the "mother of Parliaments" because it provided a model of democratic government to many other nations. The building itself—a neo-Gothic palace with one thousand rooms, one hundred staircases, and three kilometers of corridors—is very imposing and is open to the public. Debates can be watched from the vistors gallery. Question time is as much fun as chimpanzees' tea time at London Zoo!

Q: What is the difference between the Labour and Conservative parties?

British politics is essentially two-party politics, the conflict of the Labour and the Conservative parties. Traditionally, the Conservative Party is the Party for people who are rich or aspire to be rich, while the Labour party is the party for the poor, or people who feel sorry for the poor.

The Labour Party was founded in 1900. It was funded by the Trade Unions, and its mission was to fight for the rights of the ordinary working man. The party only really came into its own after a landslide victory in 1945, when it established the modern welfare state and nationalized industries ranging from coal and railways to airlines. Labour believes in the redistribution but not the creation of wealth, a stance that may have been feasible in Edwardian days (when Britain was still one of the richest countries in the world), but is quite unrealistic now, when no wealth is being created to be redistributed.

The Conservative Party traditionally represents business interests. Old-style "one-nation" Conservatives were consensus politicians, who tried to soften capitalism with compassion

非情さを和らげようとする、和を重んじる政治家
だった。それに比べて"サッチャリズム"と呼ばれ
る新たな考えを持つ保守党議員は、憐憫の情の欠
如と攻撃的な姿勢に誇りを持っている。彼らは、
経済というジャングルに住むライオンの利益を代
表していると主張する。もっとも、保守党の政治家
たちが数々の後ろ暗い取引に関与してきたことを
思えば、ライオンと言うよりは蚤のたかったハイエ
ナと形容するほうが適切かもしれない。

　保守党の支持基盤はイングランド南部で、北へ
行くほど保守党を憎む人々の割合が増えていく。
一方で労働党は、英国の"鉄錆地帯"と呼ばれる
旧重工業地帯に強い地盤を持っている。

　サッチャー夫人の活躍を目の当たりにした労働
党は、みずからを"新労働党"に改革せざるを得な
くなった。強硬左派を追放し、労働組合の力を抑
制し、人気回復を目指して政策を練り直した。
1997年に18年ぶりに労働党から首相に選出された
トニー・ブレアは、その卓越したマスコミ操作で
(それ以外にはほとんどなにもない) 知られてい
る。

　もっとも愉快でもっとも英国らしい政党は、たっ
た1つの議席を目標にしながら一度も勝ったためし
のない少数政党だろう。なかでもとりわけ魅力
に富んでいるのは、スクリーミング・ロード・スッチ
(1960年代にデビューした売れないロック歌手)と、
スッチが率いる"怪物狂乱のどうかしてる"党や、
シンシア・ペイン(昼食券と引き替えにセックスを
提供した娼館の女主人)が率いる"苦痛と快感"党
である。党員全員が塩化ビニルの下着に身を包
み、鞭を振りまわす"苦痛と快感"党は、政治に無
関心な人々の興味をかきたてることに成功してい
る。

and social responsibility. New style, or "Thatcherite" Conservatives are proud of their confrontationalism and their absence of compassion. They like to think that they represent the interests of the lions in the economic jungle. Given, however, the large number of shady deals in which Conservative politicans have been involved, they are probably better compared to flea-ridden jackals!

The Conservatives are popular in the south of England, and hated more passionately the further north one goes. Labour is very strong in the old industrial areas, Britain's "rust belt."

The impact of Mrs. Thatcher resulted in Labour reinventing itself as "New Labour." Militant left-wingers were expelled, trade union power curbed, and policies are adopted and honed to secure maximum popularity. Tony Blair, who was elected Labour prime minister in 1997 after a gap of eighteen years, is recognized as a master of media manipulation (and little else).

The most amusing—and most uniquely British—political parties are the minor ones that contest single seats but never win. Of these, Screaming Lord Sutch (an unsuccessful 1960s popstar) and his Monster Raving Looney Party, and Cynthia Payne (a madam arrested in a sex-for-luncheon-vouchers scandal) with her Payne and Pleasure Party are the most appealing. The latter, with its members all dressed in PVC underwear and brandishing whips, is able to inspire fervid interest even in the most politically apathetic.

Q: サッチャー夫人はなぜあれほど長期にわたって首相を務めることができたのか？

1979年から1990年まで保守党の党首として英国首相を務めたマーガレット・サッチャーは、英国初の女性首相であり、20世紀でもっとも長期間首相を務めた政治家だった。サッチャー夫人は、いつ終わるともしれないストライキと、100万人を超える失業者を生みだした労働党政権に辟易した選挙民の期待を担い、1979年に首相に就任した。

だが、最初の任期は成功とはほど遠いものだった。サッチャー夫人がとった財政引き締め策のおかげで倒産が相次ぎ、どうにかこうにか生きながらえていたひと握りの製造業者すら姿を消して、失業者数は300万人を超えた。夫人が再選されたのは、1982年のフォークランド紛争において強硬な姿勢を崩さなかったことにより人気が急上昇した"フォークランド効果"のおかげでしかなかった。2期目に入っても夫人はまた戦ったが、今度の敵は炭鉱の閉鎖に反対してストライキに突入した全英炭鉱労組だった。サッチャー夫人はこのストライキを、古くさい労働組合主義と自由市場経済との戦いであると象徴的に捉え、ストライキが1年にもおよんで多大な犠牲が出たにもかかわらず、けっして屈服しようとしなかった。

夫人は3度目の当選を果たしたが、欧州統合にあくまで反対し、国民の強い反発を招いた人頭税にこだわりつづけたことから、総選挙ではサッチャーの存在がマイナスに働くと判断した、みずからが党首を務める保守党によって、結局は辞任に追い込まれた。

Q: Why was Mrs. Thatcher prime minister for so long?

Margaret Thatcher, Conservative prime minister of Great Britain from 1979 to 1990, was the first woman prime minister and the longest serving prime minister of the twentieth century. She came to power in 1979 offering hope to an electorate that was tired of a Labour government that had produced endless strikes and unemployment figures totaling over 1 million.

Mrs. Thatcher's first term, however, was hardly a success. Her rigid monetarist policies caused mass bankruptcies, wiped out whatever remnants of manufacturing industry survived in the country, and pushed unemployment to over 3 million. She was only reelected because of the "Falklands effect"—a dramatic rise in popularity due to her decisive handling of the Falklands War in 1982. Her second term was again defined by conflict, this time with the National Union of Miners, who went on strike against proposed pit closures. Mrs. Thatcher saw the strike in terms of a symbolic conflict between old-fashioned trade-unionism and the liberal market economy, and did not give in, though the strike lasted a year and caused great human suffering.

Thatcher won a third-term but was finally forced to resign by her own party when her opposition to the European Union and her commitment to the highly unpopular poll tax had made her an electoral liability.

Q: サッチャー夫人は英国人に好かれていたのか、嫌われていたのか？

　サッチャー夫人は、ウィンストン・チャーチル以来もっとも有名になった英国の首相である。アルゼンチンを向こうにまわして戦ったフォークランド紛争における指導力や、(国有企業の民営化などで見せた)大胆な経済政策、ロナルド・レーガンやゴルバチョフと良好な関係を築いた外交手腕などにより、海外で高い評価を受けた。だが英国内の反応は、盲目的に夫人を崇拝するか忌み嫌うかの両極端に分かれている。

　第2次世界大戦以後の英国の政治は、国家を1つの家族と見なし、国民の和を重んじるという特徴を持っていたのに、サッチャー夫人はその和を壊したと評論家は批判する。夫人がとった政策のおかげで、長い歴史を持つさまざまな産業が崩壊して大量の失業者が生まれ、それにとって代わる新たな職種は(低賃金のサービス業をのぞけば)生まれなかった。サッチャー夫人の改革は、古いものを壊し、すでにあったものを自由化したが、新しいものはなにも生みださなかった。建設的なことはなにもやらず、結局はのらくら者や功利主義者の経済をもたらし、ひと握りの儲けすぎのヤッピーと大勢のホームレスを出現させただけだった。サッチャー夫人のおかげで、英国は思いやりのない貪欲な国家になった。

　一方でサッチャー夫人の支持者は、サッチャー夫人こそが、慢性的不況におちいり"ヨーロッパの病人"とまで呼ばれた英国が必要とした良薬だったと主張する。サッチャー夫人はごねる英国の尻を叩き、サービス業を基盤とした世界に通用する経済国家に生まれ変わらせた。労働組合を封じ込め、減税を実施し、国有企業を民営化したことは、産業界の追い風となった。世界じゅうの国々

Q: Is Mrs. Thatcher loved or hated in Britain?

Mrs. Thatcher is the most famous British prime minister since Winston Churchill. Her leadership in the Falklands War against Argentina, her revolutionary economic policies, (such as privatization), and her rapport with leaders like Ronald Reagan and Gorbachev, made her an internationally respected figure. In Britain, however, she inspires extreme feelings of either devotion or of complete loathing!

The critics say that Mrs. Thatcher broke the consensus, or the sense of a national family, that had distinguished British politics since World War II. Her policies caused massive job losses in traditional industries, but provided no new jobs, (other than low-paid service jobs) in their place. She made social divisions worse, with both the economic gap between rich and poor, and North and South widening under her government. Her reforms consisted in the destruction of the old and the liberalization of the pre-existing, but not in the creation of anything new. She did nothing constructive, and ultimately created a "spiv" economy full of a few overpaid yuppies and armies of homeless people. She made Britain a greedier and a less compassionate place.

Her fans, on the other hand, say that she was just the medicine that Britain—nicknamed "the sick man of Europe" because of its poor economic performance—needed. She pulled a kicking and screaming Britain into the new global, service-based economy. Her triumph over the unions, her tax cuts, and her privatizing of state industries created a favorable climate for business. Her policies were imitated over the world, and they made Britain the number one target for inward investment in Europe.

がサッチャー夫人の政策を真似、英国はヨーロッパ最大の投資先となった。

サッチャー夫人の政策をどう見るかはさておいても、彼女の強烈な個性を否定することは誰にもできないだろう。かつてフランスのミッテラン大統領は、「サッチャー夫人の目はカリギュラのようで、口元はマリリン・モンローのようだ」と評し、ロシア人は夫人を"鉄の女"と呼んだ。世論調査の結果を横目でうかがいながら政策を決める政治家が多すぎる昨今、信念に基づいて国を治める政治家の存在は新鮮だった。

Q: 新労働党とは？

労働党は1980年代から1990年代初頭にいたるまで、カリスマ性に富むサッチャー夫人を擁する保守党と対照的に力と方向性を見失い、内部分裂していた。国民にとって労働党は、1970年代の英国経済の衰退を思い起こさせる存在だった。つまり、保守党は低い税率、労働力の柔軟性、民営化、経済成長などを意味したのに引き替え、労働党は過酷な重税、強すぎる労働組合、ストライキ、国営化などを意味したのである。

労働党はまた、政治家の人間的魅力という点でも保守党にひけをとっていた。労働党の指導者たちは広く国民に訴えかける魅力に欠けていた。ウェールズ出身のおしゃべりなニール・キノックも、善良なスコットランド人のジョン・スミスも、労働党の地盤が弱い豊かなイングランド南部で票を集めることはできなかった。上品ぶった人間が寄り集まった国家では、救世主は地方からは現れないのである。

Regardless of how one feels about her policies, the strength of her personality cannot be denied. President Mitterrand of France said she had "the eyes of Caligula, and the mouth of Marilyn Monroe." The Russians nicknamed her the "Iron Lady." And in an age when so many politicians make up their policies based only on the latest opinion polls, it is refreshing to find someone who governed from conviction.

Q: What is New Labour?

In the 1980s and early 1990s the Labour Party looked weak, lost, and divided compared to the Conservatives, with their charismatic leader, Mrs. Thatcher. In the public mind Labour was associated with all the failings of the 1970s British economy. So while Conservative meant  low taxes, flexible labor, privatization, and economic growth, Labour meant punitively high taxes, overpowerful trade unions, strikes, and nationalization.

Labour was also losing the war of personality politics. Its leaders lacked broad appeal. Neither a Welsh windbag like Neil Kinnock, nor a decent Scotsman like John Smith could gather the votes where Labour was weakest—in the prosperous south of England. In a land of snobs, the Messiah could not hail from the provinces.

　　1994年5月にジョン・スミスが心臓発作で急死すると、トニー・ブレアが労働党の新たな党首となった。ブレアはアメリカ政界の熱心な信奉者で、テレビ時代の政治は見てくれがすべてだということを知っていた。そこでピーター・マンデルソンの手を借りて、彼は労働党のイメージ改革に着手した。

　　労働党は大事業の国営化という公約を破棄し、（党の財政のかなりの部分を担う）労働組合の影響力を抑え込んだ。急進左派を追放し、国防の強化、減税、国営企業の民営化など、対立する保守党の政策をことごとく公約として掲げた。

　　化粧直しは成功し、1997年の総選挙の結果、18年間政権党の座に居座りつづけて息切れしていた保守党に労働党は圧勝した。フランス、スペイン、アメリカ、オーストラリアの各国ではすでに、政権をとり、引き続き権力を握りつづけるために、政府は理想主義を捨て、経済界寄りの実利的な政策を採用しはじめており、保守派と革新派の政策は変わりばえのしないものになっていた。新労働党も、これと同じ現象が英国で起きたものにすぎない。

Q: 王室の役割とは？

　　英国は立憲君主国家である。つまりエリザベス2世は国家元首であり、国軍の最高司令官であり、英国国教会の首長ではあるが、実際上の権限は持たず、政治的に中立でなければならないのである。

　　女王の役割は、現在ではほぼ形式的なもののみに限られている。女王は国会の開催を宣言し、爵位を授与し、諸外国の元首をもてなし、海外においては英国の外交官の役割を果たす。

When John Smith died suddenly of a heart attack in May 1994, Tony Blair became the new leader of the Labour Party. A devoted student of the American political scene, Blair knew that politics in the television age was all about how one was perceived. With the assistance of Peter Mandelson, he set about revamping the image of the Labour Party.

The party's commitment to nationalize major industries was jettisoned, and the power of the trade unions (who provide much party financing) was curbed. Militant left-wingers were expelled from the party, and Labour committed itself to strong defence, low taxes, privatization—essentially to all the policies of its opponents, the Conservatives!

The face-lift worked, and in 1997 the Labour Party won a landslide victory, defeating the Conservative Party which had run out of steam after eighteen years in power. France, Spain, the United States, and Australia had already seen a convergence of the policies of left and right, with socialist parties abandoning their ideology and adopting pragmatic, pro-business policies in order to get into, and then hang onto, power. New Labour is simply the British version of this phenomenon.

Q: What is the role of the monarchy?

Great Britain is a constitutional monarchy. This means that although Queen Elizabeth II is the head of state, commander-in-chief of the armed forces, and head of the Church of England, she has no executive power and is obliged to be politically neutral.

The queen's role is now largely ceremonial. She takes part in the opening of parliament, distributes honors, receives visiting heads of state and acts as an ambassador for Britain abroad.

　女王は積極的に政治に関わることはないが、国会を通過した法案は女王が署名しなければ成立することができない。また、企業の役員が会長に事業報告を行わねばならないのと同じように、首相は毎週国情を国王に報告しなければならないことから、国王は首相になんらかの影響力をふるっていると言うことができる。サッチャー夫人（社会を分断するような政策をとった）と女王（"国家は1つの家族"という温情主義的な信念を持つ）の仲がきわめて悪かったのは周知の事実である。

　女王の子どもたちが成長して悪さをするようになるまでは、王室は英国という統一国家の象徴として尊敬されていた。身近なところでは王室は家族の価値を象徴していたし、マクロなレベルでは政党間の小競り合いを超えた安定と伝統を表していた。

　だが1980年代に入ると、日々の暮らしにも困窮している一般国民を尻目に買い物や休暇や浮気にうつつを抜かしている王室一家を叩けば販売部数が伸びることに、タブロイド紙が目をつけた。マスコミの報道によって国民は王室に厳しい目を向けるようになり、王室の存在意義を疑問視する声が出はじめた。

　皮肉な見方をすれば、王室の存在価値はなくなったわけではなく、変化しただけだと言うこともできるだろう。王室はもはや、国民が誇りとし、見習おうとする手本ではなくなった。アメリカの大統領と同じように、王室一家もいまや、視聴率を最大限に伸ばそうとする多国籍メディア企業の餌食にされる、現代情報産業の商品の1つにすぎないのだ。

　アメリカでは、一般市民が数百万人の視聴者の前で悩みを語り、視聴者と胸の痛みを分かち合う『オプラ』というトーク番組が爆発的な人気を博している。英王室が現在あてがわれている役割も

The queen has no active political power, but acts of Parliament cannot become law until they have received her signature. More importantly, she has some informal influence over the prime minister, because he or she must report to her on the state of the nation every week, like a director reporting to the chairman of the board. It is well known that Mrs. Thatcher (with her socially divisive policies) and the queen (with her paternalistic, "one-nation" view) got on extremely badly.

Before the queen's children grew up and started misbehaving the monarchy was respected as a unifying symbol of Britain. On a micro level it represented family values. On a macro level, it represented stability and tradition, something above the squabbles of party politics.

Since the 1980s the tabloid press found it could sell more copies by attacking the royal family as parasites who spent their time shopping, holidaying, and fornicating, while the man-in-the-street was having a hard time even making a living. Public opinion has consequently become more hostile, and the value of the monarchy has been brought into question.

Looking at the issue cynically, the value of the royal family has not dwindled, merely changed. It is no longer a model family for citizens to be proud of and to emulate. Like the American president, the royals are now just a bit of the modern information economy to be manipulated by multinational media companies seeking to maximize ratings.

In America the talk show "Oprah"—a public therapy session where ordinary people talk about their troubles and share their pain with an audience of millions—is phenomenally successful. The British royal family now has had a similar role

これに似ている。王室は集団ヒステリーの標的であり、大人になろうとしない国家の欲求不満のはけ口にされているのだ。

女王一家がマスコミという動物園のなかで、一見立派な金の檻に入れられて惨めな暮らしを送っていることを思えば、王室の廃止をもっとも強く望んでいるのは彼ら自身と言えるかもしれない。

Q: 近年王室の人気が落ちたのはなぜか?

この10年間に王室は数々のスキャンダルを提供してきた。そのほとんどはチャールズ皇太子とダイアナ妃にまつわるものだったが、王室のほかの面々も多少の貢献は果たしてきた。下にそのスキャンダルを時間順に書きだしてみよう。

チャールズとダイアナは1981年7月に結婚した。2人は新婚旅行中に早くも、お互いに共通点がなにもないことを発見した。ダイアナは過食し、食べたものを吐きだし、そのために劇的に痩せることによって、満たされない気持ち(およびチャールズの古くからの愛人カミラ・パーカー＝ボウルズへの嫉妬)を表現した。彼女はまた、階段から転げ落ちたり、手首を切ったり、キャビネットのガラス扉に体当たりしたりして、何度も自殺をはかった。チャールズとダイアナが2人揃って姿を見せることはほとんどなくなり、たまに2人で一緒にいても態度はよそよそしかった。

チャールズとダイアナの結婚生活が破綻の危機に瀕しているという噂は長いあいだ囁かれていたが、エリザベス女王が"さんざんな年"とラテン語で感想を述べた1992年、いっせいに問題が噴きだした。この年、アン王女はマーク・フィリップス大尉と離婚し、アンドリュー王子もセーラ妃(テキサ

thrust upon it. It is a focus of mass hysteria, an emotional purgative for an infantilized nation.

Given the miserable lives that the royal family live in their gilded cages in the media zoo, one suspects that they are probably among the most fervent supporters of the movement to abolish themselves.

Q: What has caused the recent decline in the popularity of the royal family?

There has been a mass of royal scandals in the last ten years. The majority of these centered on the Prince and Princess of Wales, though other members of the royal family made some efforts of their own. Below is a small chronicle of scandal.

Charles and Diana were married in July 1981. As early as their honeymoon the couple discovered they had nothing in common. Diana expressed her unhappiness (and her jealousy for Charles's longtime mistress, Camilla Parker-Bowles) by overeating, then making herself vomit, with the result that she lost weight dramatically. She also attempted suicide on a number of occasions by throwing herself downstairs, cutting her wrists, and crashing into a glass-fronted cabinet. The couple seldom appeared together and looked distant when they did so.

For a long time it had been rumored that the Wales's marriage was on the rocks, but everything came to a head in 1992, a year that the Queen would refer to as her "*annus horribilis*" ("horrible year" in Latin). In that year Princess Anne divorced Captain Mark Phillips, the Duke of York separated from his wife the Duchess of York (who had been photographed sun-

スの財政顧問に足の指をしゃぶらせながらトップ
レスで日光浴している写真を撮られた)と別れ、ロ
ンドン郊外に建つ王室の別宅ウィンザー城が火災
に遭い、4000万ポンドの被害が出た。しかも国民
は、ウィンザー城の補修に税金を使うことを許そう
としなかった。

　だがこれら一連の事件も、チャールズとダイア
ナが引き起こした問題の前には色あせた。1992年
の夏、ダイアナが電話でジェイムズ・ギルビーと交
わした会話の内容がマスコミに流れた。ギルビー
がダイアナを「愛しい人」と呼ぶ一方で、ダイアナ
は王室のことを「このいまいましい家族」と形容し
たり、彼女の「つばめ」であるジェイムズ・ヒューイ
ット大尉のために服を買ってあげると言ったりし、
2人はマスターベーションの話をした。その後、ダ
イアナとチャールズの不幸な結婚生活を詳しく綴
った『ダイアナ妃の真実』がアンドリュー・モートン
によって出版された。こうなると、もはや形だけの
結婚生活を続けることはほぼ不可能になり、1992
年12月、時の首相ジョン・メージャーは、チャール
ズ皇太子とダイアナ妃は離婚すると発表した。

　だが、話はそれだけでは終わらなかった。1993
年1月、チャールズと彼の愛人の会話がすっぱ抜か
れ、そのなかでチャールズは彼女の「スラックスの
なかで暮らしたい」と言っていたことが発覚した。
さらに、ダイアナの乗馬教師だったジェイムズ・ヒ
ューイットが、ダイアナとの情事をハーレクイン・ロ
マンスばりに生々しく詳細に書き綴った告白本を
出版した。チャールズとダイアナはそれぞれテレ
ビに出演し、失敗に終わった結婚生活について心
情を吐露した。その間ダイアナは、イギリスのラ
グビーチームの主将と不倫関係におちいり、主将
の妻が離婚を申し立てた。

　1996年に入ると、チャールズ皇太子とダイアナ

bathing topless while having her toes sucked by a Texas financier), and there was a fire at Windsor Castle, the royal residence just outside London, that caused £40 million of damage which the tax-payer refused to pay.

All these events paled compared to the Wales's problems. In the summer of 1992, transcripts of phone conversations between Diana and James Gilbey were published. He called her "Squidgey," while she referred to the royal family as "this fucking family," spoke of buying clothes for her "toyboy" Captain James Hewitt, and discussed masturbation. Andrew Morton then published *Diana, Her True Story* in which the facts of her unhappy life with Charles were detailed. After this it was almost impossible for the pretence of a marriage to be maintained, and in December 1992 John Major, the prime minister, announced that the Prince and Princess of Wales would separate.

This, however, was not the end. In January 1993 conversations between Charles and his mistress were published in which he expressed a desire to "live inside her trousers." James Hewitt, Diana's riding instructor published a book detailing their affair in lurid detail and in language worthy of a Harlequin romance. Both Charles and Diana went on TV to talk about their failed marriage. Diana, meanwhile, had an affair with the captain of the English rugby team, which resulted in his wife filing for divorce.

In 1996 the marriages of Charles and Diana and the Duke

妃の離婚と、アンドリュー王子とセーラ妃の離婚が成立した。ダイアナはハロッズ百貨店のオーナーの息子、ドディ・アルファイドと交際を始めたが、1997年8月31日、ベンツでパリのセーヌ河畔を飛ばしている最中に自動車事故で死亡した。

彼女の死が神の心を鎮めたのか、愛憎入り交じった奇妙な共生関係をマスコミと築いてきたダイアナが去って以来、王室は落ち着きを取り戻している。

Q: ダイアナ妃はなぜあんなに人気があったのか？

最新の通信機器が、結局は無意味な情報を大量に送りだすだけに終わることは、ハイテク時代の大いなる皮肉である。ゴシップに飢えた地球村のなかでは、ダイアナ妃がどんな服を着ていたかとか、彼女が誰とつき合っているかといったことが、もっとも価値あるニュースとして扱われる。1997年に彼女が自動車事故で急死したとき、たくさんの人々が衝撃を受けたが、それは、マスコミを介して彼らもダイアナの人生に参加していたからにほかならなかった。彼らはダイアナ妃の不貞や健康問題、あるいは自殺未遂などの事情を、じつに詳しく知っていた。ひょっとしたら自分の配偶者のことよりも、よく知っていたかもしれない。

『ピープル』紙（本書の執筆に際して調査のために筆者がそのホームページを訪ねたタブロイド紙）は、読者とダイアナ妃の関係を率直にこう表現している。「1981年7月29日の豪華絢爛な結婚式以後、もしダイアナ妃が幸せに暮らしていたら、この15年間は退屈な歳月になっていたことだろう。だが私たちは、悲しくも見応えのあるメロドラマを堪能させてもらうことができた」ダイアナはハーレクイン・ロマンスの世界へ市民を誘い、何億という人々が、

and Duchess of York were dissolved. Diana began a relationship with Dodi Al-Fayed, son of the proprietor of Harrods department store, which ended when their Mercedes crashed on August 30, 1997, as they sped along by the River Seine in Paris.

This death seemed to appease the gods, and things have been going better for the royal family since Diana, with her strange symbiotic love–hate relationship with the media, left the scene.

Q: Why was Princess Diana so popular?

It is the great paradox of the high-tech age that the most sophisticated communications equipment ultimately serves only to provide a stream of the most trivial information. In the gossip-hungry global village, questions such as what Princess Diana was wearing, or whom she was dating were treated as matters of the utmost newsworthiness. When she died unexpectedly in a car crash in Paris in 1997 many people felt a sense of shock simply because, thanks to the media, they had participated in her life. They knew about her infidelities, her health problems, her suicide attempts—more intimate details, perhaps, than they knew about their own spouses.

People (an American tabloid whose website I visited while researching this book) is quite honest about the relationship that its readers had with Diana. "If she had lived happily ever after the July 29, 1981, wedding extravaganza…the last fifteen years would have been ever so boring. Instead we got to wallow in a sad but spectacular soap opera." She provided an entree into a world straight out of a Harlequin romance for hundreds of millions of people who fed on her dramatic experience from the safety of their armchairs.

彼女の波乱に満ちた人生を安全な高見から見物
した。

　ダイアナの短かった生涯を眺めた時、どんな人
でもそのいずれかの時期に共感できる部分を見い
だすことができた。彼女は清らかな花嫁、ショッ
ピングに目がないお嬢さん、きらびやかなプリンセ
ス、夫に裏切られた妻、子どもを愛する母親、献
身的な慈善事業家、そして最後に離婚経験者と、
じつにさまざまな役割を演じた。

　ダイアナ妃の死に際して英国のマスコミは、そ
れまで感情を表すことのなかった英国人が（人前
ですすり泣き、花輪や詩やテディベアをケンジン
トン宮殿に供えた）ようやく感情を素直に表現でき
るようになったと、心理学用語を駆使した摩訶不
思議な記事を競って掲載した。

　私は個人的には、他人の死を——しかも直接知
っていたわけでもなかった人物の死を、感傷的な
自己礼賛の小道具にすべきではないと思う。エイ
ズ患者や地雷の被害者の窮状を社会に訴えたダ
イアナ妃はたしかに功績も残したが、彼女の死が
いかに悲劇的で、また早すぎたとしても、彼女は
超人的な英雄でもなければ天使でも聖者でもなか
った。むしろ、人間の持つ弱さこそが彼女の魅力
だったのである。

At different stages in her short life Diana offered something for everyone to identify with. She was in turns the virgin bride, the irresponsible, shop-till-you-drop playgirl, the glamor princess, the betrayed wife, the loving mother, the heroic charity worker, and finally the divorce survivor.

When Princess Diana died the British press was full of bizarre psycho-babble articles in which the once-inhibited British public (openly crying, bringing wreaths, poems, and teddy bears to Kensington Palace) was congratulated for having learnt to express its emotions.

Personally I don't think anyone's death, let alone that of someone one does not even know directly, should be treated as a cause for narcissistic and maudlin self-congratulation. Princess Diana did some good things, such as bringing public attention to the plight of AIDS sufferers and landmine victims, but however tragic her premature death, she was not superhuman, an angel, or a saint. Her appeal was in her very human weaknesses.

HISTORY

歴史

Q: エリザベス1世のどこがそんなにすごかったのか？

エリザベス1世の前国王メアリーと、その夫でカトリック教徒のスペイン王フェリペは、イングランドにカトリックを復興させるべく強硬措置をとり、メアリーの治世には多くのプロテスタントが焼き殺された。このためにメアリーは"ブラディ(血まみれ)・メアリー"と呼ばれている。

これと対照的に、エリザベスはイングランドに平和をもたらすことに心を注ぎ、1558年に即位すると、穏健なイギリス国教制度を確立した。だがこのためにカトリック教会系の大国スペインと対立することになり、エリザベス統治時代のイングランドはスペインと常に戦いを繰り広げていた。

英国の水夫は頻繁にスペイン人居留地を攻撃し、南米のスペイン領から財宝を積んで帰国する船を襲った。1588年に(嵐に助けられて)サー・フランシス・ドレイクが100艘を超える船と3万人の水兵を擁するスペインの無敵艦隊をうち破ると、海上におけるイングランドの覇権は揺るぎないものとなった。

女王のために戦った水夫たちは、女王のために探検にも繰りだした。サー・フランシス・ドレイクは"金の雌鹿号"で世界じゅうを航海した。植民地が建設され、詩人で歴史家、探検家、軍人であり、煙草やジャガイモを英国にもたらしたサー・ウォルター・ローリーは、北アメリカに建設した植民地を、処女王エリザベスに敬意を表して"ヴァージニア"と名づけた。

軍事、商業の両面における成功に伴い、文学も花開いた。マーロウやシェイクスピアの戯曲も、エドマンド・スペンサーの叙事詩『神仙女王』も、エリザベスの時代のものである。

Q: What was so remarkable about Queen Elizabeth I?

Queen Elizabeth I's predecessor, Mary, and her Catholic husband, Philip of Spain, were determined to restore Catholicism in England, with the result that Mary's reign was distinguished only by the number of the Protestants who were burned at the stake. Hence her nickname of "Bloody Mary."

Elizabeth, by contrast, was set on bringing peace to England, and so established a moderate Church of England when she acceded to the throne in 1558. This, however, immediately set her in opposition to Spain, the dominant Catholic power, and Spain and England were at war throughout her reign.

British seamen were forever attacking Spanish settlements or capturing ships laden with treasure from Spain's South American colonies. England's dominance at sea was confirmed by the destruction of the Armada, a huge force of over 100 ships and 30,000 men that was defeated by Sir Francis Drake's fireships (with the help of a storm) in 1588.

The same sailors who fought for the queen also explored for her. Sir Francis Drake circumnavigated the globe in the *Golden Hind*. Colonies were established, with Sir Walter Raleigh—poet, historian, explorer, soldier and first importer of tobacco and potatoes—calling the American colony he established "Virginia" in honor of Elizabeth, the Virgin Queen.

Military and commercial success was accompanied by a flourishing of literature. The dramatic works of Marlowe and Shakespeare, and Edmund Spenser's epic poem, *The Faerie Queen*, all date from Elizabeth's reign.

Q: 大英帝国はどのように形成されていったのか？

　　大英帝国は19世紀末には巨大国家となっていた。領地は地球の5分の1にまたがり、世界人口の4分の1が英国旗のもとに暮らしていた。しかし、大英帝国が巨大化したのは計画に基づいた結果というよりはむしろ偶然の産物であり、あれほどの途方もない大きさにまで膨らんだのは19世紀後半のたった50年間のことだった。

　　初期の大英帝国は、英国商人の交易路を確保するためや、英国の船舶を守る海軍基地として使用するためのいくつかの戦略港と島から成っていた。アフリカの黄金を手に入れるための交易路だったゴールドコースト（現在のガーナ）は前者の例であり、地中海から大西洋に通じる要衝で1704年に英国が占領したジブラルタルは後者にあたる。

　　18世紀になり、英国の海軍力と経済力が増すにつれ、大英帝国は膨張を始めた。商業利益をさらに拡大するために、東インド会社がインドの各地方を次々に直轄地にしていく一方で、キャプテン・クックはオーストラリアを英国に加えた。

　　ネルソン提督がトラファルガーの海戦（1805）でフランス艦隊を破ってから第1次世界大戦にいたるまで、英国は世界一の海軍力を誇った。英国はさらに植民地を増やし、1819年にはシンガポールを、1842年には香港を手に入れた。1840年にはニュージーランドを植民地としたが、これは英国にとって重大な転機となった。ニュージーランドを併合したのは、必要だったからではなく、フランスに先を越されないためだったのである。

　　それ以降、植民地は飛躍的に拡大していき、ヨーロッパの列強は低開発国の天然資源と市場を求めて争った。1857年には英国はインド全土を統治

Q: How did the British Empire develop?

By the end of the nineteenth century, the British Empire was colossal. It spanned one-fifth of the globe, and a quarter of the world's population lived under the British flag. Nonetheless the empire grew much more through accident than through design, and only swelled to its final, monstrous size in the last half of that century.

In its early phase the empire consisted of a few strategic ports and islands which existed either to provide British merchants with access to tradeable goods, or as naval bases from which British shipping could be protected. The Gold Coast (modern-day Ghana) which provided access to the gold of Africa is an example of the former. Gibraltar, which commands the passage from the Mediterranean to the Atlantic and was captured by the British in 1704, is an example of the latter.

In the eighteenth century, as British naval and commercial power grew, the empire began to expand. The East India Company, in order to further its commercial interests, was bringing more and more of India under its direct control, while in 1770 Captain Cook claimed Australia for the crown.

After the Battle of Trafalgar (1805), in which Nelson defeated the French Fleet, Britain enjoyed uncontested naval supremacy until World War I. She began to acquire more colonies. Singapore was added in 1819 and Hong Kong in 1842. The acquisition of New Zealand in 1840 was a turning point. It was annexed not because the British wanted it, but in order to stop the French getting it first!

Thereafter the empire expanded by leaps and bounds, with the European powers struggling to control both the natural resources and the markets of the less-developed world. India

下に置き、19世紀末になると、英国がアフリカ大陸に所有する植民地をつなげばアフリカ大陸を南北に縦断することができるほどだった。

1898年に起きたオムデュルマンの戦いは、19世紀帝国主義の姿をまざまざと伝えてくれる。この戦いでは1万人のスーダン人が機関銃で蜂の巣にされたが、英国側が失った兵士の数は、なんと26人にすぎなかったのである。

1852年の時点で、ディズレーリは早くも、植民地は「わが国の首にくくりつけられた石臼」と発言しており、第2次世界大戦が終結するころになると、巨大帝国を支えられるだけの資力が英国にはないことが明白になった。植民地のほとんどは戦後まもなく独立を承認されたが、分断されたインドとパキスタンの場合に見られるように、独立のあとには激しい戦闘が待っていた。

旧植民地諸国はいまでは"英国連邦"に所属している。

Q: 産業革命はなぜ英国で始まったのか？

産業革命は18世紀後半に英国で始まった。当時英国はすでにその豊かさでヨーロッパの羨望の的となっていた。1688年の名誉革命によって王室の力が弱まり、上流階級が強い力を持つようになると、上流階級が求める実際的、商業的な利益を第1に考えた政策がとられた。海上の覇権を握った英国はヨーロッパ最大の貿易国となり、植民地は、紅茶や砂糖、香辛料などの天然資源や、輸入して再輸出するための奴隷を英国にもたらしてくれると同時に、商品の市場にもなってくれた。英国は国内市場も巨大で、人口は増えつづけ（なかでもロンドンは欧米一の大都市だった）、交通網も発達していた。

became a crown colony in 1857, while later that century Britian was controlling a swathe of Africa running the whole length of the continent.

The 1898 the Battle of Omdurman provides a neat snapshot of late nineteenth-century imperialism. Ten thousand Sudanese were cut to pieces by machine guns, while the British sustained losses of only twenty-six men!

In 1852 Disraeli had spoken of the colonies as a "millstone around our necks," and after World War II it became clear that Britain was no longer sufficiently rich to support her vast empire. Most colonies were granted independence soon after the war, though independence was often followed by savage fighting, as that between partitioned India and Pakistan.

The former countries of the empire now belong to the "British Commonwealth."

Q: Why did the Industrial Revolution take place in Britain?

The Industrial Revolution took off in Britain in the late eighteenth century. By then the country was already the envy of Europe for its prosperity. The "Glorious Revolution" of 1688 had increased the power of the gentry at the expense of the monarchy, and government policy was dictated by the practical, commercial interests of the upper classes. Britain's dominance at sea had made her the greatest trading nation in Europe, and her colonies provided her with natural resources such as tea, sugar, spices, and slaves for import and reexport, while themselves providing a market for goods. Britain also had a large domestic market, an expanding population, (particularly in London, the largest city in the Western world) and excellent transport links.

　　1769年にリチャード・アークライトが水力紡績機の特許をとったのを契機に、今日われわれが当然のことと受けとめている際限なく拡大する経済のひな型が生まれた。アークライトは水力機械を組み合わせることによって工場というシステムを発明し、綿花産業から産業革命が始まった。

　　18世紀に入ると鉄鋼や鉄道などの重工業が生まれ、ここでもまた英国人の手になる発明品が世界を引っ張っていった。ジェイムズ・ワットの蒸気機関は炭坑から水を汲みだすのにも使われ、工場の動力としても活用された。サー・ハンフリー・デイヴィーが発明した安全灯により、石炭をより安全に掘りだせるようになった。そうやって採掘した石炭を、ロバート・スティーブンソンが設計した画期的な"ロケット号"が牽引する列車が、線路を介して効率的に流通させた。

　　1870年代になり、化学や電気などのより洗練された新産業が台頭すると、当時まだ他国を大きく引き離し、とりわけ財政的には豊かだった英国も、高度に訓練された労働力を有するアメリカ、ドイツ、日本などの新興産業国に追い抜かれはじめた。

Q: イングランドとアイルランドの関係は？

　　イングランドとアイルランドの関係はあまりにも不幸なために、たびたび日本と韓国の関係と比較されてきた。

　　プロテスタントのイギリス人がローマカトリックのアイルランドを征服して移り住んだのは、16世紀後半のことだった。それからの100年間、イングランドからの侵略者に対する反乱は、武力によって鎮圧された。1740年代と1840年代の飢饉においても、アイルランド原住民の多くが命を落とした（19世紀には脱出してアメリカへ移住する選択肢もあった）。

The breakthrough to the ever-expanding economic model which we now think of as normal came with Richard Arkwright, who patented his spinning machine in 1769. Grouping the water-powered machines together, it was he who invented the factory system, and the Industrial Revolution was initially driven by the cotton business.

In the early nineteenth century, heavy industry—iron, steel, and railways—took off, again with British innovations setting the pace. James Watt's steam engine was used to pump water out of mines as well as to power factories. Coal could be mined more safely with Sir Humphry Davy's Safety Lamp. This coal could then be efficiently distributed by rail, pulled by trains based on the design of Robert Stephenson's breakthrough *Rocket*.

By the 1870s, as new and increasingly sophisticated industries like chemicals and electricity appeared, Britain, though still preeminent, especially in finance, was beginning to be outperformed by newly industrializing countries with highly trained work forces like the United States, Germany, and Japan.

Q: What is the relationship between England and Ireland?

The relationship between England and Ireland is such an unhappy one that it is often compared to the relationship between Japan and Korea.

Roman Catholic Ireland was originally conquered and settled by the Protestant English in the late sixteenth century. In the following century, revolts against the England invaders were crushed with great brutality. A large proportion of the native population also died in famines in the 1740s and 1840s. (Emigration to America was available as an escape route in the nineteenth century.)

1916年、英国の支配に対して反乱（"復活祭蜂起"と呼ばれている）が起きた。これは鎮圧されたが、アイルランド共和国軍（IRA）はなおもゲリラ活動を続け、その結果1921年にアイルランドはプロテスタント系住民が多数を占める北アイルランドと、カトリック系が住むアイルランド自由国の2つに分割され、アイルランド自由国は1949年にアイルランド共和国となった。

現在北アイルランドで起きている紛争は、1968年の事件に端を発している。この年、王立アルスター警察隊は、少数派であるカトリック教徒による差別抗議のデモ隊を弾圧した。この事件をきっかけにして、50年間休眠状態にあったIRAが目を覚まし、プロテスタント系住民のさまざまな民間警護隊と小競り合いをはじめた。1969年に入ると、英国は軍隊を進駐させて紛争をおさめようとし、1972年にはアイルランド議会の権限を奪ってロンドンの直轄支配下に置いた。

政治的な解決を求めようとする試みはことごとく失敗に終わり、暴力は爆弾テロという形で英国本土にも飛び火し、1984年には保守党大会に出席中のサッチャー夫人と閣僚がIRAに命を狙われた。

ジョン・メージャーが保守党の首相に就任すると、1991年、16年ぶりに対立各派が交渉のテーブルにつき、1997年に労働党から首相に就任したトニー・ブレアも、和平の気運を維持して解決策を模索しようと意欲を見せた。

"ブレア効果"のおかげで問題は順調に解決に向かうかに見えた。民間警護隊の大半は停戦に合意し、英国軍も監視をゆるめ、服役者は釈放され、武器は撤収され、新たな議会が設立された。ところが1998年8月、自分たちこそが正当なIRAだと主張するIRAの少数派強硬グループがオーマで

In 1916 there was a revolt (called the Easter Rising) against British rule. This was suppressed, but persistent guerilla attacks by the Irish Republican Army (IRA) resulted in the 1921 partition of the country into the largely Protestant Northern Ireland, and the Catholic Irish Free State, which in 1949 became the Republic of Ireland.

The current disturbances in Northern Ireland began in 1968. Demonstrations by the Catholic minority against discrimination were repressed by the Royal Ulster Constabulary. The IRA, which had been dormant for fifty years, revived to confront various Protestant paramilitary groups. In 1969 British soldiers were sent in to control the conflict, and in 1972 the Irish Parliament was superseded by direct rule from London.

Attempts at finding a political solution failed, and the violence crossed over into the British mainland in the form of bombing campaigns, most notably in the IRA's attempts to assassinate Mrs. Thatcher and the government at the Conservative Party conference in 1984.

In 1991, under the Conservative government of John Major, the various parties were brought to the negotiating table for the first time in sixteen years, and Tony Blair, elected Labour Prime Minister in 1997, came into office determined to keep up the momentum and find a solution to this problem.

Thanks to the "Blair effect," the peace process appeared to be going well. Most paramilitary groups had agreed to a cease-fire, the British army presence was being reduced, prisoners were being released, weapons were being decommissioned, and a new assembly was established. However, in August 1998 a bomb attack in Omagh by a splinter group of the IRA,

爆弾テロに訴え、29人の命を奪ったことから、和
平交渉は水泡に帰した。北アイルランドにどんな
未来が待ち受けているのか、本書が出版される現
時点では誰にもわからない。

Q: 英国はいつ超大国でなくなったのか？

　超大国としての地位を失ったことに英国が気づ
いた決定的な瞬間は、1956年のスエズ動乱の際
に訪れた。このとき、スエズ運河の国有化に対抗
して、サー・アンソニー・イーデン首相は英仏連合
軍を送り込んだ。しかし、アメリカの支援は得られ
なかった。ポンド相場は下落し、イーデンは大恥
をかかされ、軍の撤退を余儀なくされた。砲艦外
交を楽しむ特権はアメリカのみにあることを、アメ
リカ人はこのときまざまざと見せつけたのだった。
アメリカの国務長官ディーン・アチソンは、英国は
「帝国を失い、まだ新たな役割を見つけていない」
と名言を吐いた。
　スエズ動乱に象徴される軍事力と対外的影響
力の喪失に伴い、経済も衰退しはじめた。英国の
工場は他のヨーロッパ諸国に比べて大戦による被
害が少なかったため、1950年代後半は輸出景気
に湧いた。しかしこの繁栄は幻にすぎず、旧式の
工場、労働者の教育不足、無能な経営陣、劣悪な
労使関係などにより、1960年代から1970年代にか
けて企業がつぎつぎに倒産していった。ホバーク
ラフトやコンコルドなどの英国が生んだ画期的な
技術も、商売としては成功しなかった。戦後の経
済政策の失敗は、デニス・ヒーリー蔵相が1977年
に国際通貨基金に39億ドルもの資金貸与を願いで
る事態となったことと、"不満の冬"と呼ばれた
1978年から1979年にかけての相次ぐストライキと
に如実に示された。

calling itself the true IRA, claimed twenty-nine lives, putting the peace process in jeopardy. At the time of going to press no one knows what the future may hold for Northern Ireland.

Q: When did Britain cease to be a superpower?

The defining moment that Britain realized it was no longer a superpower was in the Suez Crisis of 1956. In reponse to the nationalization of the Suez Canal, Sir Anthony Eden, the prime minister, had sent in an Anglo-French military force. The Americans, however, refused to back him up. Sterling came under enormous selling pressure, and a humiliated Eden was forced to order a withdrawal. The Americans made it clear that indulging in gunboat diplomacy was now a privilege that the U.S. reserved for itself alone. Hence Dean Acheson's famous observation that Britain "had lost an empire and not yet found a role."

The loss of military and diplomatic power symbolized by Suez was accompanied by economic decline. Since British factories had sustained less damage in the war than their continental counterparts, exports boomed in the late 1950s. This was an illusory success, and in the 1960s and 1970s Britain lost ground as antiquated plant, an ill-educated work force, incompetent managers, and appalling labor relations drove more and more businesses into the ground. Even British technological breakthroughs, such as the Hovercraft and Concorde, were commercial flops. The economic failure of the postwar period was symbolized by Dennis Healey, the Chancellor of the Exchequer, having to beg for a loan of $3.9 billion from the International Monetary Fund in 1977, and the strike-infested "winter of discontent" in 1978–79.

　そんな国家の衰退を、サッチャー夫人が食い止めたと言われている。しかし、31人の犠牲者を出した1987年のキングスクロス駅の火災をはじめとする人災や、何億ポンドも横領したロバート・マックスウェルのような野心に満ちた実業家のスキャンダルが頻発するのを見るにつけ、最大限の利潤を生もうとする余り安全性や公正さがないがしろにされていることが実感されて、躍動的で起業家精神に富む新文化というキャッチフレーズも虚ろに響くばかりである。

Mrs. Thatcher claimed to have reversed the country's decline. But the rhetoric about a new, dynamic, and entrepreneurial culture was undermined by manmade disasters such as the 1987 fire at King's Cross Station which left 31 people dead, and scandals involving high-flying businessmen like Robert Maxwell, who embezzled hundreds of millions of pounds. Such episodes suggested that the new prosperity was superficial, with profits maximized without regard for safety or honesty.

経済

ECONOMICS

Q: 英国はどんな産業に秀でているのか？

　　ソニーの電気製品、トヨタの車、マイクロソフト
のソフトウェア、マクドナルドのハンバーガー——
世界じゅうどこへ行っても、日本とアメリカの活発
な経済活動の疑いようのない証拠を目の当たりに
することができる。ところが、英国の政治家が主
張する"経済の奇跡"の証拠を見つけるのは、悲し
いかな相当に困難だ。

　　英国の製造業が衰退したことは、どんなレトリッ
クを用いてもごまかすことのできない明白な事実
である。1950年代末には、英国はオートバイ、自
動車、工作機械、船舶の製造の各分野において世
界を引っ張っていた。しかしいまでは、これらの
産業は休眠に近い状態にある。

　　それでも、なかには英国が得意とする産業も存
在する。リオ・ティントジンクのような採鉱会社、シ
ェルやブリティッシュ・ペトロリアムのような石油企
業、兵器を製造しているヴィッカーズなどは、いず
れも大英帝国時代から連綿と続いてきた企業だ
が、いまでもそれぞれの分野で世界の先頭を走っ
ている。メディア産業においても、英国は平均以
上の活躍を見せている。『フィナンシャル・タイム
ズ』や『エコノミスト』を発行しているピアソン社は
その好例だし、ビートルズやローリング・ストーン
ズの曲を配給しているEMIやヴァージンのような
レコード会社も元気だ。バーガーキング、ギネス、
ジョニー・ウォーカーといった世界的に有名な食
品、飲料会社や、ホテルチェーンのホリデイ・イン
のような娯楽企業の多くも英国企業である。伝統
的に科学に強い国にふさわしく、グラクソ・ウェル
カムやスミスクライン・ビーチャム（日本でも"コン
タック"がよく売れている）などの薬品会社はとり
わけ優秀だ。航空産業を見ても、ヴァージン・アト

Q: What businesses is Britain good at?

Sony electronics, Toyota motorcars, Microsoft software, McDonalds' hamburgers—wherever you go in the world, you are confronted with irrefutable evidence of the dynamism of the Japanese and American economies. Finding any such evidence to support the claims of "economic miracles" made by British politicians is, alas, much harder.

Britain's decline as a manufacturer is a simple matter of fact that cannot be reversed by any amount of rhetoric. In the late 1950s Britain was one of the world's leading producers of motorcycles, automobiles, machine tools, and ships. Now it is barely active in any of these fields.

There are, nonetheless, areas of strength in the British economy. Mining companies such as Rio Tinto Zinc, oil companies like Shell and BP, and arms manufacturers like Vickers, all of which date from Britain's imperial past, continue to be world leaders. Britain's performance in the media industries, too is above average. Consider Pearson, which publishes *The Financial Times* and *The Economist*, or record companies such as EMI and Virgin, which distribute the songs of the Beatles and the Rolling Stones. Many world-famous food, drink, and leisure brands such as Burger King, Guinness, Johnnie Walker, and Holiday Inn hotels are managed by British holding companies. Appropriately for a country with a strong scientific tradition, Britain is an exceptionally strong performer in pharmaceuticals, with firms like GlaxoWellcome and Smith Kline Beecham (whose Contac is a best-seller in Japan). In air transport, Virgin Atlantic Airways is a pioneer of new forms of service, while British Airways, in sharp contrast to JAL or Air France, regularly posts impressive profits.

ランティック航空は他に先駆けて新しい形のサービスを提供したし、英国航空は日本航空やエールフランスとは対照的に、つねにかなりの黒字を計上している。

英国経済界のなかで突出した業績をあげているのは、国家経済の15パーセントに相当する経済活動を行っているロンドンの金融業界だろう。ロンドンの金融の心臓部"シティ"は、規制緩和、国営企業の民営化、市場への非干渉主義といったサッチャー夫人がとった政策から恩恵を受けた。ある意味では英国の近年の繁栄は、金融機関がありとあらゆる英国企業を――ときにはみずからも含めて――海外の投資家に売り払う一種のガレージセールによって得られたものがほとんどだと言えるかもしれない。

"シティ"は資産を動かしているだけで新しいものはなにも生みだしていないと、マスコミはたびたび批判してきた。ストライプのシャツを着て受話器に向かってがなりたてるだけで何十万ポンドも稼ぐ人間がいるかと思うと、重労働に明け暮れる人々の労働意欲はおおいにそがれるというものである。それでも、若い遣り手たちが資産を動かすためには、誰かがその資産を生みだしてやらねばならない。しかし結局のところ、金融サービス業が雇用できる従業員数はきわめて限られている。大銀行は数千人の従業員を雇用するが、製造業は数十万人規模の働き口を生みだすのだから。

製造業と言えば、このところ英国ではちょっとした製造業ブームが起きている。経営者が英国人だった当時は低い生産性に悩まされていた工場が、経営陣が外国人に入れ替わった途端に大きく成長しはじめたのである。英国はまた、海外の多国籍企業が欧州工場を設立する際の絶好の建設候補地にもなっている。ありがたいことに、安い労働

By far the most significant sector in the British economy is the London-based financial services industry, which accounts for 15 percent of the total economy. The City, the financial heart of London, benefited from Mrs. Thatcher's policies of deregulation, privatization, and strict noninterference in the market. In a sense, much of the recent prosperity in Britain has been generated by a kind of garage sale in which financial institutions sold British firms of all kinds—occasionally including themselves—to foreign bidders.

The City is often criticized in the press for merely moving assets around, and not creating anything new. On a psychological level, the knowledge that one can be paid hundreds of thousands of pounds just for shouting down the phone and wearing striped shirts is a serious disincentive to doing any more laborious kind of business. Someone, however, has to create the assets for the whiz kids to move around. Ultimately, the amount of employment that financial services can create is very limited. A huge bank will employ thousands of workers, but a manufacturer will employ hundreds of thousands.

On the subject of manufacturing, there has been a small British revival recently. Factories that were plagued by low productivity when under British management have registered great gains after being sold to foreign management. Britain has also become the most popular place for foreign multinationals to locate their European factories. Lured by cheap labor, government grants, the absence of any domestic producers demand-

力、政府の援助、保護を求める国内企業の欠如、有利な税金などの諸条件に魅力を感じた多国籍企業が、英国人がわざわざみずからの手で生みだす気になれない産業を興してくれている。

Q: 南北問題とはなにか?

イングランド南部の住人は昔から北部のことを、L・S・ラウリの絵画や、チャールズ・ディケンズの小説『ハード・タイムズ』に描かれている典型的な工場の街、コークタウンのような、陰気な人々の住む煤けた場所だと考えてきた。ディケンズは、コークタウンを次のように描写している。

「そこは赤煉瓦と機械と高い煙突の街だった。煙突からは絶えずくねくねと煙が立ちのぼり、けっして途切れることがない。街のなかには黒々とした運河と、いやな匂いの染料で紫色に染まった川が流れ、おびただしい数の建物にはまった窓という窓が震えて一日じゅうカタカタと音をたてており、数え切れないほどの小さな通りにはよく似た人たちが住み、同じ時刻に家を出て、そっくりな歩道に瓜二つの靴音を響かせながら、同じ職場に向かっている」

また「北部の生活は厳しい」という伝統的なことわざがある。

単純労働に従事する人たちばかりが住む煤煙で真っ黒になった工場の街よりももっと悲惨なものがあることが、最近明らかになった。それは、工場という工場が閉鎖され、誰1人としてどんな仕事にもつくことができない街である。その対比は、『フル・モンティ』という英国映画のオープニングシーンに鮮やかに描かれている。

産業革命の中核をなした石炭、鉄鋼、鉄道、紡績、造船などの19世紀の産業は、すべて北部に集

ing protection, and a favorable tax environment, multinational firms are kindly setting up the businesses that the British cannot be bothered to set up for themselves.

Q: What is the North–South divide?

The north of England is traditionally imagined by southerners to be a grimy place full of dour people, as depicted in the paintings of L. S. Lowry, or in the following description of Coketown, a typical milltown of the 1840s, from Charles Dickens's novel *Hard Times*.

"It was a town of redbrick…of machinery and tall chimneys, out of which interminable serpents of smoke trailed themselves for ever and ever and never got uncoiled. It had a black canal in it and a river that ran purple with ill-smelling dye and vast piles of building full of windows where there was a rattling and a trembling all day long…and it contained many small streets, inhabited by people like one another, who all went in and out at the same hours with the same sound upon the same pavements, to do the same work."

There is also a traditional saying "It's grim up North."

Recently it has become clear that there is something much worse than these smoke-blackened factory towns full of people doing repetitive jobs, and that is towns full of closed factories with no opportunities for anyone to do any work at all. This contrast is skillfully shown in the opening scenes of the British movie *The Full Monty*.

The old nineteenth-century industries of coal, iron and steel, railways, cotton, and shipbuilding that formed the core

中していた。これらの産業は19世紀末には早くも
翳りを見せはじめていたが、第1次世界大戦と第2
次世界大戦のあいだに出現した軽工業は、ミッド
ランドと呼ばれるイングランド中部地方と南部地方
のみに興ったために、北部に生じた空白を埋めら
れるものはなにもなかった。そのため、北部は英
国のどの地方よりも失業率が高く、世帯収入が低
く、生活保護の受給者数の多い土地となった。

　政治家も実業家も1980年代初頭までは、北部の
ことを心配するだけの社会的責任感を持ち合わせ
ていた。しかしいまや自由経済という呪文——サ
ービス業こそがこれからの産業であり、市場介入
はアナルセックスと同じくらい不自然な行為で、弱
者は敗北して当然だ——が、この問題を忘れるた
めの便利な口実になっており、北部に工場を建設
するという任務は、安い労働力に惹かれてヨーロ
ッパ進出をうかがう多国籍企業に一任されている。

Q: 英国経済をプラス思考で眺めたら？

　英国経済は1980年代に生まれ変わったと信じ
る人々は、次のように英国経済を褒め讃える。
　英国は世界経済をリードする7ヵ国の一員（イタ
リアの下でカナダより上）であり、英国の海外資産
はアメリカに次いで世界第2位で、年間1000億ポン
ド近くを稼いでいる。
　ヨーロッパにおいても、英国は海外からの投資
をもっとも多く受け入れており、ソニー、トヨタ、フ
ォード、ゼネラルモーターズなどの多国籍企業の
工場を招致し、数々の企業のヨーロッパ本社所在
地となっている。金融業と銀行業においても、ロ
ンドンはヨーロッパ内でもっとも重要な金融センタ
ーであり、東京—ロンドン—ニューヨークを結ぶ

of the Industrial Revolution were all concentrated in the North. These industries had already begun to decline even in the late nineteenth century, but the new light industries that sprung up between the two World Wars were all located in the Midlands or in the South, so nothing was created to replace the void in the North. Consequently, in the North unemployment is higher, household incomes are lower, and the number of recepients of welfare payments higher than other regions of the United Kingdom.

Until the early 1980s, politicians and businessmen still retained enough sense of social responsibility to worry about the North. Now the mantras of the free market—that services are the way forward, that market-intervention is an unnatural act on a par with sodomy, and that the weak must go to the wall—provide a convenient pretext for forgetting about the whole problem and building factories in the North is now left to multinational corporations looking for cheap labor and an entry into Europe.

Q: What is the positive view of the British economy?

People who believe that the British economy was born again in the 1980s tend to praise it as follows.

Britain is the top seven economies in the world (below Italy but above Canada), while British overseas assets are second only to the United States, bringing in nearly £100 billion of income annually.

In Europe Britain attracts more investment from overseas than any other country, hosting factories of multinational giants like Sony, Toyota, Ford and General Motors, and it is the European headquarters of many others. In finance and banking, London is not just the most important center in Europe, but it is a part of the twenty-four-hour Tokyo–London–New York axis, and the number one currency trading

24時間軸の1つで、通貨の取引高では世界一である。シェル、ブリティッシュ・ペトロリアム(石油)、ユニリバー(消費財)、ブリティッシュ・テレコム(通信)、英国航空(旅行)などの英国企業は、フォーチュン誌の世界500社リストの上位にランクされている世界的な企業だ。また、リチャード・ブランソンが経営するヴァージン・グループやボディショップに代表される、独創的で起業家精神に富んだ企業も成功をおさめている。

1970年代に英国をヨーロッパの頭痛の種にした慢性的な問題は解消した。物価上昇率(1975年には25パーセントに達した)は抑制された。労働組合の力は抑え込まれ(サッチャー夫人が炭鉱労働者のストライキを粉砕したことに象徴される)、労働力は他のヨーロッパ諸国より安くなり、融通も利くようになった。

製造業に寄りかかった経済から、付加価値をつけたサービス業を主体とする経済への転換を、ヨーロッパ諸国のなかで一番うまく成し遂げたのは英国である。全労働人口の71パーセント強が、いまではサービス業に従事している。英国はまた、失業率も課税率もEU諸国のなかでもっとも低く、どこよりも健全な国家財政を誇っている。

1980年から1996年にかけての英国経済の伸びは、日本にこそおよばなかったものの、アメリカ、イタリア、ドイツ、フランスの各国よりもめざましかった。さらに『エコノミスト』誌の最近の調査によると、英国は世界一事業を展開しやすい国に、競争力では世界第7位にランクされている。

Q: 英国経済をマイナス思考で眺めたら?

前ページで述べた英国経済の楽天的な評価に興味をそそられ、経済の黄金郷にあやかろうと英

center in the world. Many British firms such as Shell and British Petroleum (oil), Unilever (consumer goods), British Telecom (telecoms), and British Airways (travel) are world-class businesses high in the ranks of the global Fortune 500 list. There is also a flourishing creative and entrepreneurial culture typified by Richard Branson's Virgin Group or the Body Shop.

The chronic problems which made Britain the despair of Europe in the 1970s have been overcome. Inflation (which reached 25 percent in 1975) has been brought under control. Union power has been curbed (symbolized by Mrs. Thatcher's defeat of the miners' strike), and labor is cheaper and more flexible than on the continent of Europe.

Of all European countries, it is Britain that has most successfully transformed itself from an economy dependent on basic manufacturing to a value-added service economy. Over 71 percent of the total work force is now working in the service sector. Britain can also boast the lowest unemployment rate, the lowest tax rates, and the most healthy government finances of any major EU country.

Between 1980 and 1996 the British economy grew faster than the U.S., Italian, German, or French economies—only the Japanese economy grew faster. And in recent surveys by *The Economist* magazine, Britain was ranked number one for business environment and number seven for global competitiveness.

Q: What is the negative view of the British economy?

If a Japanese person were to be inspired by the upbeat assessment of Britain's performance on the previous page to make a

国を訪ねた日本人がいたとしたら、その人は驚くべき光景を目にすることになるだろう。荒れはてたビル、古色蒼然たる地下鉄、でたらめな間隔でやってくる電車やバス、共産主義華やかなりしころ以来お目にかかったことのない無能さと態度の悪さを兼ね備えたスタッフが働くホテルや店、通行人に金をせびるホームレスのティーンエイジャーが群れる街路……。

英国人は自国の経済をきわめて甘い基準で評価していることを、とくに日本人のような良識ある人々は理解する必要がある。ストライキが頻発した70年代と、工業が衰退し失業者が街にあふれた80年代を経験した英国人は、なんらかの経済活動を行うことができさえすればそれで満足なのである。国家が破綻しなかったことそのものが奇跡なのだ。なるほど日本にはソニーが、アメリカにはマイクロソフトが、ドイツにはダイムラー・クライスラーがあるかもしれないが、英国のささやかな企業が潰れもせずに存続できれば、それはもう充分に賞賛すべき出来事なのである。

英国経済は数値だけ見ればかなりの規模だが、人口が多いことと、世界で最初に工業化された国家だという事実を考慮すれば、感心するほどのものではない。国内総生産全体ではなく1人あたりの国内総生産を見てみると、英国は世界の22位にランクされているにすぎない。英国の国内総生産は1人あたり1万8849ドルだが、これは日本の半分以下で、ドイツやアメリカの3分の2であり、フランスの5分の4にすぎず、かつては英国の統治下にあったシンガポールや香港（いずれも2万3000ドル内外）をも下まわっている。

金融業界はたしかに元気だが、適度な給与を稼げる働き口を全国にまんべんなく生みだす製造業

pilgrimage to what he imagined to be an economic Eldorado, what a surprise he would get! Seedy buildings, primitive subways, trains and buses coming and going seemingly at random, hotels and shops with staff who combine incompetence and surliness in a way not seen since the palmy days of the communist bloc, streets infested with homeless teenagers begging for money. . .

It is important, especially for common sense people like the Japanese, to understand the far-from-strict criteria by which the British judge their own economy. After the strikes of the 1970s, and the deindustrialization and mass redundancies of the 1980s, the British are only too pleased with themselves if they can achieve any economic activity at all. The absence of catastrophe is itself a miracle. The Japanese may have Sony, the Americans Microsoft, and the Germans Daimler-Benz, but if a small British company can contrive to even exist, that is cause enough for self-congratulation.

Britain may still have a relatively large economy in absolute terms, but, considering the size of the population and the fact that the country was the first in the world to industrialize, this is hardly surprising. Looked at not in terms of overall GDP, but in terms of per capita GDP, Britain is only number twenty-two in the world rankings. Britain's $18,849 per head is less than half of Japan, two-thirds of Germany or the US, four-fifths of France, and it ranks below the former colonies of Singapore and Hong Kong (both in the $23,000 range).

Finance is undeniably flourishing, but it creates only a small number of high-paid jobs focused on London, unlike

と異なり、金融業は高給を約束されたひと握りの働き口をロンドンで生みだすだけである。世界一流と評判のいい英国企業も、一部分だけが英国のものである場合が多く（シェルもユニリバーも半分はオランダ）、英国が植民地を支配していた時代に手に入れた特権に支えられていたり（ブリティッシュ・ペトロリアムの掘削権、英国航空の航空路）、民営化された時期が早かったために過大な注目を浴びた公共事業（ブリティッシュ・テレコム）にすぎなかったりする。また、起業家がマスコミの注目を浴びるのも、たんに起業家があまりにもめずらしいためにすぎない。

次に、英国がサービス業に強いという主張を検討してみよう。"サービス"という言葉を聞けば、ラップトップ・コンピュータを携えた、世界じゅうから意見や分析を求められるコンサルタントを思い浮かべるかもしれないが、サービス業にはハンバーガーを引っ繰り返したり近所の子どものお守りをしたりといった仕事も含まれているのである。サービス業の雇用が増えているのは、製造業が衰退していることの裏返しでしかない。英国にわずかに残された製造業における働き口は、英国企業ではなく多国籍企業からもたらされている。無能な経営陣とストライキに目がない労働者がお定まりの衝突を繰り返す従来の英国企業（労使ともに世界経済という大きな舞台で戦うよりも、階級闘争というけちな芝居を好んだ）は、潰れるか乗っとられるかして姿を消した。集団で働くことが英国人には生まれつきできないのだということを、いまでは誰もが認めている。

高度の知識を身につけた人々は、弁護士、銀行家、会計士、証券ブローカーなどになって金を稼ぐことができる。だが、英国経済の全体図はこの国の天候と同じでとてつもなく暗い。

manufacturing companies which can create large numbers of reasonably paid jobs spread out over the entire country. British firms that are praised as leaders are often only partly British (both Shell and Unilever are half Dutch), or they derive much of their strength from benefits they secured when Britain was an imperial power (drilling concessions for BP, air routes for British Airways), or they are no more than utilities which received disproportionate attention because they were privatized early (British Telecom). Entrepreneurs receive media attention only because they are so rare.

As for boasts about Britain's strength in services. "Services" may evoke images of consultants with laptops, their opinions and analysis in demand all around the world, but service jobs also include plenty of "Macjobs" like burger-flipping and baby-sitting. A service employment boom is just the flipside of failure in production. Such little manufacturing employment as exists in the U.K. is now found in factories belonging not to British firms, but to multinationals. Traditional British companies, in which incompetent managers and strike-prone workers engaged in ritualistic conflict (both sides preferring the petty pantomime of class conflict to the larger drama of the global economy) have been wiped out or taken over. The pathological inability of the British to work together in a large unit is an accepted fact.

Highly educated individuals can make money in Britain as lawyers, bankers, accountants, or stockbrokers. The general picture, is, however, like the weather—unrelentingly grim!

その他

MISCELLANY

Q: 英国のタクシー運転手はなぜあれほど有能なのか？

　日本人と英国人にはたくさんの共通点がある。どちらもあまり背が高くなく、社交下手で、自分を嘲うことのできるユーモアのセンスを持ち合わせており、アメリカ人のような単純な楽観主義から自由である。だが同時に、両国民がまるで正反対で、一方が優れているのに他方は救いようがない領域も存在する。たとえば、英国のテレビ番組は世界一と評価されているが、日本のテレビは微笑ましくもくだらないものでしかないと見なされている。日本の製造業は世界一だが、英国の製造業は世界最悪だ。英国と日本が対極に位置するもう1つの領域が、タクシーの運転手である。

　外国人が書いた日本に関する本の多くがタクシー運転手の驚くべき無能さに言及しており、日本のタクシーは、実質よりも形式を重んじる東洋の伝統を具現化しているように見える。日本のタクシーの車両は染み1つなく磨かれ、ドアは自動で、自動車電話や領収書を印刷する機械まで備えている。運転手は純白の手袋をはめ、ネクタイを締めている。ところが、Aという地点からBという地点へどうやって行けばいいかについてはなにも知らず、料金がどんどんあがるのもおかまいなしにうろうろ走りまわったり、停車して地図とにらめっこしたりする。

　日本では、東京に出てきたばかりの人が翌日からタクシーの運転手になるのもむずかしいことではなさそうだ。必要なのは運転免許証だけである。これと対照的にロンドンでは、タクシーの運転手は高度な訓練を受けた専門家である。調査表

Q: Why are British taxis so good?

The Japanese and the British are in many ways similar peoples. They are both, for instance, of rather short height, rather socially awkward, capable of self-mocking humor, and free from the naïve optimism of the  American. At the same time, there are also ways in which the two peoples are complete opposites, and certain things at which one nation is good while the other is hopeless. British TV, for instance, is respected as the best in the world. Japanese TV meanwhile is regarded as no more than charmingly ridiculous. Japanese manufacturing is the best in the world, British manufacturing, the worst. The quality of taxi drivers is one such area where the British and the Japanese are polar opposites.

Many foreign-authored books on Japan comment on the startling incompetence of Japanese taxi drivers, who seem to provide a classic example of the Oriental preference for form over substance. The cab is spotlessly clean. It has an automatic door, a cell phone, and a machine for printing receipts. The driver wears shining white gloves and a tie—but he has absolutely no idea how to get from A to B, and worse, seems to feel no guilt about driving around aimlessly or stopping to consult a map as the fare gets higher and higher.

In Japan it is not hard to come up to Tokyo and start working as a taxi driver the next day. All you need is a driving license. In London, by contrast, the taxi driver is a highly trained specialist. Only after spending two or three years buzzing around London on a scooter with a check list acquiring "the knowl-

片手にスクーターにまたがり、2、3年かけてロンドンの街を隈なく走りまわって、企業オフィス、クラブ、美術館、病院、劇場、映画館などの所在地と、どうすればそれらの場所へ速く行けるかを学ばないかぎり、タクシー運転手の免許をとることはできない。

もっとも、いったん免許をとってしまえば、ロンドンのタクシー運転手の振る舞いは傍若無人である。無茶なUターンをし、信号を無視し、ほかのドライバーを怒鳴りつけ、自転車に体当たりする。客を一刻も早く目的地に届けるためには手段を選ばないのだ。観光客のみなさん、お気をつけあれ。タクシー運転手は外国人嫌いで気の短いことで知られている。タクシーに乗る前には、目的地をちゃんと発音できるようにしておくのが身のためだ。

Q: 英国が多くの発明家を生んだのはなぜか？

英国は国内総生産で見ると世界で6番目の国家にすぎないが、ノーベル賞の受賞者はアメリカに次いで世界第2位である。つまり、国家規模から考えると不釣り合いなほど、英国には独創的な科学者が多いのである。

日本の歴史や科学の教科書にも、著名な英国人科学者の名を数多く見つけることができる。微積分を考えだした（工学、力学、重力の理論も生んだ）ニュートンを思いだしてほしい。水力紡績機を発明して産業革命を起こしたサー・リチャード・アークライトや、ロケット号を造って蒸気機関車の基本構造を確立したロバート・スティーヴンソンの名もご存じだろう。

時代が下ってからも、英国人は次々に重大な発見を成し遂げてきた。サー・アレキサンダー・フレミングは、世界初の抗生物質、ペニシリンを発見

edge"—learning where all the offices, clubs, museums, hospitals, theaters, and cinemas are, and all the shortcuts to get to them—will he get his license.

Once licensed, however, the London cabbie is a law unto himself. He does U-turns, shoots traffic lights, yells insults at other motorists, and knocks cyclists over—anything to get the customer to his destination faster! Tourists beware! The cabbie is often a xenophobe with a very short temper, so make sure you can pronounce the name of the place you want to go before you get in the cab!

Q: Why does Britain produce so many inventors?

Britain is only the world's sixth largest developed economy in GDP terms, but it has the second highest number of Nobel Prize winners after the United States. In other words, the number of original scientific minds in Britain is disproportionately high.

There are many famous British scientists and inventors who appear in Japanese history and science textbooks. Think of Newton, who invented calculus (and produced theories of optics, mechanics, and gravitation); Sir Richard Arkwright, who set off the Industrial Revolution with his water-powered spinning machines; and Robert Stephenson, whose *Rocket* established the principles of the steam locomotive.

In more modern times British inventors have continued to make important breakthroughs. Sir Alexander Fleming invented penicillin, the world's first antibiotic. Alan Turing formalized

した。アラン・チューリングはコンピュータ理論を
創りだした。SF作家としても有名なアーサー・C・
クラークは衛星通信を発明している。フランシス・
クリックはDNAの構造を共同で解明したし、最近
ではイアン・ウィルムット博士が成熟した羊のクロ
ーンに成功している。

　英国に発明家が多い理由としては、無知な迷信
を温存することに熱心なカトリック教会と袂を分か
ったこと、経験に基づく独創的な思考と研究を重
んじる伝統があること、ケンブリッジ大学キャベ
ンディッシュ研究所をはじめとする優れた研究機
関があること、などを挙げることができるだろう。

　それでも、ふんぞり返っている余裕は英国には
ない。研究には資金が必要であり、発明品を巧み
に商品化することによってのみ金は生まれるので
ある。そして、商売こそまさに英国人が苦手とす
る領域なのだ。英国における発明品は、往々にし
て他国で大量生産される結果に終わる。英国の
電機メーカーEMIは世界で初めてスキャナーを造
った。ところが、それを巧みに製品化したのは日
本だった。

　英国企業が製造業から撤退し、国家が貧しくな
ればなるほど、産業界でも大学でも研究費は削ら
れていくに違いない。研究者の給与はますます減
り、その結果いよいよ多くの英国人科学者が報酬
の恵まれた他国へと流れていくだろう。

　電話を発明し、AT&T（アメリカ電話電信会社）
を設立したアレキサンダー・グラハム・ベルは、21
歳の若さで北米に移住した。これこそ、利口な英
国人科学者の多くが現在も目指していることであ
る。

the concept of the theoretical computer. Arthur C. Clarke, in addition to being a successful science fiction author, also invented the communications satellite. Francis Crick co-discovered DNA, and, most recently, Dr. Ian Wilmut successfully cloned an adult sheep.

Factors that account for the high number of British inventors are the country's early separation from the Catholic church, with its vested interest in maintaining ignorant superstitions, a strong tradition of independent, empirical thought and inquiry, and the existence of great institutions, such as the Cavendish Laboratories at Cambridge University.

Britain, however, cannot afford to be conceited. Research requires money, and money is generated by the successful commercial exploitation of inventions. This is what the British are not good at. Things invented in Britain often end up being commercially mass-produced elsewhere. EMI, a British electronics company, produced the world's first scanner. But it was successfully commercialized by the Japanese.

As British companies withdraw from manufacturing and the country grows ever poorer, research budgets both in businesses and at universities will inevitably shrink. Researchers will receive less and less attractive salaries, so more and more British scientists will choose to emigrate to countries where they are better rewarded.

Alexander Graham Bell, the Scottish-born inventor of the telephone, and the founder of AT&T emigrated to North America when he was twenty-one years old. This is what most clever British scientists aspire to do now, too.

Q: "英国ファッション"という表現は撞着語法か？

　英国人の大多数は、"階級社会"と呼ばれる社会に暮らすことにうんざりしている。彼らは他人より"上品"で"金持ち"と思われることを極度に恐れながら生きている。そのために、わざとみすぼらしい格好をして、"労働者階級"の人間に見られるように努力する。地味な服装をしたがるこの傾向は、資力の欠如によってさらに強化される。ファッション・デザイナーにとっては喜ばしくない社会だ。

　英国人デザイナーのなかでもっともその名を知られているのは、ポール・スミス（紳士服）とヴィヴィアン・ウェストウッド（婦人服）だろう。

　1971年にブティックを開店したポール・スミスは海外にも進出し、全世界で営業する店舗の総売り上げは年間1億7100万ポンドに達しており、日本では200もの店舗を展開している。彼は英国式にていねいに仕立てた服に奇抜なポップアート的味づけをほどこして強烈な"ブリティッシュ・キッチュ"感覚を生みだし、大成功をおさめた。彼は"英国らしさを最大限に表現したい"と語っており、こと服装に関しては、英国人はほかの国民ほど保守的でないと考えているようだ。

　"フェティッシュ"の流行の先駆けとなり、下着をアウターウェアとして着ることを提案したヴィヴィアン・ウェストウッドは、現代のファッション界にもっとも影響力を持つデザイナーの1人と絶賛されている。しかし、商売上の業績のほうは成功とはほど遠い。つい最近まで売り上げは年間60万ポンドにすぎなかったし、ウェストウッド自身も公営住宅に住んで自転車で仕事に出かけていたのである。ファッションを商売として成功させる術を学ぼうとしなかったウェストウッドは、どこか自己破壊的なその姿勢のおかげで金銭的には恵まれなかった

Q: Is the expression "British fashion" an oxymoron?

The majority of British people are very unhappy to live in what they have been repeatedly told is a "class society." They live in terror of being thought to be "posher" or "richer" than anyone else. Consequently they try very hard to appear "working class" by dressing badly. This tendency to shabby dressing is further exacerbated by lack of money. All in all, it is not good news for fashion designers.

The most famous British designers are Paul Smith (for menswear) and Vivienne Westwood (for women's wear).

Paul Smith started out in 1971, and now has an annual turnover of £171 million with shops all over the world, including an astonishing 200 outlets in Japan! Using a quirky pop art wit he added zest to Britain's strong traditions of tailoring to create his own unique "Brit-kitsch" style. He is on record as saying that he wanted to "maximize the Britishness" of his creations, and believes British people are less conformist in how they dress than other nationalities.

Vivienne Westwood, who pionneered trends like fetish, and underwear as outerwear, is hailed as one of the most influential designers of modern times. Nonetheless, she can hardly be called a success from a business point of view. Until recently her turnover was only about £600,000 a year, and she lived in a council house and went to work on a bicycle. Her slightly self-destructive refusal to master the practical aspects of fashion as a business have kept her on the margin, but then, this is only appropriate for the mind behind punk!!

が、パンクの思想を体現する彼女は、まさにそうあるべきなのかもしれない。

最近、英国の若いデザイナー2人がフランスのブランドに引き抜かれ、大きな話題になった。ロンドン出身でタクシー運転手を父親に持つアレキサンダー・マックィーンがジバンシィの社内デザイナーになり、ジョン・ガリアーノがディオールのデザイナーになったのである。このとき新聞各紙は、アイデアの枯れはてたフランス人が、大胆で独創的な英国人にとうとう泣きついてきたと、勝ち誇った論調の記事を競って掲載した。言うまでもないことだが、海外で活躍する優秀なデザイナーが2人いる程度では英国ファッション界の隆盛と呼ぶことはできないし、(審美的な観点ではなく)商売という点から見れば、大騒ぎするほどのことではない。

英国人は自国の産業を維持できないほど無能になり、自国の製品を買うことができないほど貧しくなったために、ダックス・シンプソンやアクアスキュータムなどの歴史ある英国ブランドの多くが海外の企業に買収されていった。

それでも靴に関しては、英国ブランドの人気はいまなお高い。ドクター・マーテン、チャーチ、シェリーズなどのブランドが世界的な成功をおさめているのは疑いようもない事実である。

Q: なぜ1960年代の英国はそんなにおしゃれだったのか？

1960年代の飛んでるロンドンは流行の最先端を突っ走っていた。英国から発信されたものはどんなものでも"おしゃれ"だった。音楽界にはビートルズとローリングストーンズが君臨していたし、映画ではショーン・コネリーを起用したジェームズ・ボンドのシリーズがブームだった。テレビではい

Recently much has been made of two young British designers being head-hunted by French fashion houses. Alexander McQueen, son of a London taxi driver, became in-house designer for Givenchy, and John Galliano for Dior. The newspapers were full of articles crowing triumphantly about how the French had run out of inspiration, and had to come begging for help from the dynamic and creative British. Of course, two successful designers working in another country hardly constitute a fashion industry, so there was little to get excited about from a business (rather than an aesthetic) point of view.

As the British become too incompetent to manage their own businesses and too poor to buy their own products, many traditional "British" brands such as Daks Simpson and Aquascutum have been bought by foreign companies.

Shoe making is one area of fashion where Britain remains strong. Brands like Dr. Marten, Church, and Shellys are unequivocal international successes.

Q: Why was 1960s Britain so cool?

In the 1960s Swinging London was the mecca of fashion. Everything British was "in." In music there were the Beatles and the Rolling Stones; in movies the James Bond series with Sean Connery; on TV there were now classic shows like "The Prisoner" and "The Avengers"; in the West End there were the dramas of Peter Schaffer (best known for *Amadeus*, which he

まや古典作品となった『プリズナー・No.6』や『秘
密探査員ノート』が放映され、ウェストエンドへ行
けばピーター・シェイファー（1970年代に執筆した
『アマデウス』で有名）の芝居やジョー・オートンの
笑劇を観ることができたし、自動車業界では、い
まも変わらぬ人気を誇るミニや、官能的でパワフ
ルなEタイプジャガーが生みだされていた。

　『クラッシュ』の著者J・G・バラードによると、
1940年代から1950年代にかけての英国は「偏狭で
閉塞していた」が、1960年代半ばになると「変化が
起き、5年間というもの、階級制度は存在しないか
に見えた」という（もっともバラードは、1970年代初
頭になると「英国はかつての偏狭で閉塞した階級
意識旺盛のせせこましい社会に逆戻りした」とつ
け加えている）。

　1960年代は、戦後の生活苦から這いだした英国
が、1970年に入ってオイルショックに見舞われ、製
造業の基盤崩壊と大量の失業者に苦しむようにな
るまでの、うわべだけは繁栄と希望に満ちた“小
春日和”だったと解釈すべきだろう。ある意味で
1960年代は、ビクトリア朝時代の英国経済のたく
ましさと、現代消費社会の小生意気な魅力とが混
じり合った時代だった。伝統と現代が遊び心たっ
ぷりに混ぜ合わされ、誰もが豊かになっていくよう
に見えたこの時代には、社会階級は固定されたも
のだと見なすことから生じる階級間憎悪を捨て去
ることができたのである。

　1960年代は、英国が（いまや性癖となった）悲観
主義や無気力状態におちいる前に、つかの間光
を放った時代と言えるだろう。

Q: SASとはなにか？

　英国人は自国の軍隊に誇りを持っている。戦争

wrote in the 1970s) and the farces of Joe Orton; while in auto design there was the ever-popular Mini and the sensuously powerful Jaguar E-Type.

J. G. Ballard, author of *Crash*, commented that while Britain in the 1940s and 1950s was "narrow, limited, confined," in the mid-1960s "change took place, [and] for five years the class sytem did not seem to exist." (He adds, however, that by the early 1970s "we were back in the same closed, confined, class-conscious little society.")

The 1960s is best interpreted as an artifically prosperous and hopeful "Indian summer," when the country had emerged from the austerity of the postwar years but had not yet encountered the oil shocks and consequent collapse of the manufacturing base and employment of the 1970s. In a sense the 1960s combined the economic robustness of Victorian Britain with the cheeky charm of modern consumer culture, The "trad" and the "mod" were mixed in a witty, playful way, and, since everyone seemed to be getting more prosperous, old class hatreds—based on assumptions of social immobility—could be thrown out of the window.

The 1960s was very much the swan song of Britain before it sank into (its now habitual) pessimism and directionless apathy.

Q: What is the SAS?

The British are proud of their armed forces. Wars and military

や軍事パレードは、"われわれがかなり得意とする
分野だ"と英国人は言う。そんな英国の軍隊のな
かでも、SAS（テロ対策特殊部隊）はもっとも有名
で高い評価を受けている部隊である。

SASは選抜奇襲部隊で、世間の注目を避ける努
力をしたにもかかわらず、1979年にロンドン西部
のイラン大使館に首尾よく突入したのをきっかけ
に世界的にその名を知られることになった。事件
の際、SASの兵士は大使館正面の壁をロープで伝
い降り、窓ガラスを破って内部に突入してテロリ
ストを射殺し、その一部始終がテレビで生中継さ
れたのである。人目を避ける最良の方法とはとう
てい言えなかった。

SASはあまりにも非情で有能であるために、実
在の兵士というよりは映画に出てくる勇敢なヒー
ローのようである。『マスターキートン』という日本の
漫画にも、日本人とイギリス人を親に持ち、かつて
はSASの隊員だった保険調査員が登場して、SAS
で身につけた戦闘技術やサバイバルテクニックを
駆使している。こんな漫画があるのを見ても、
SASが世界の人々の興味をどれほどかきたててい
るかがわかるだろう。

SASは1941年、デイビッド・スターリングという若
い将校によってアフリカにおいて設立された。ス
ターリングは人員と装備を極力減らし、奇襲部隊
を最大限に活用することが重要だという信念を持
っていた。そこで彼は60人の部隊を5人からなる
独立したグループに分け、そのそれぞれが独自に
練った作戦をみずからの判断で実行に移せる仕
組みを作った。彼らは北アフリカで目を見張る実
績をあげ、とりわけ飛行場の襲撃に成果をあげた
が、スターリング自身は捕らえられて2年間の捕虜
生活を送っている。

pageants are, they like to say, "one of the things we're actually rather good at." In the British army, no regiment is more respected or better known than the SAS, or Special Air Service.

The SAS is an elite commando force that, despite its best efforts to keep out of the limelight, has become extremely well known since the successful storming of the Iranian embassy in West London in 1979. The siege, in which members of the SAS abseiled down the front of the building, smashed through the windows and massacred the hostage-takers, was televised live. Hardly the best way to keep a low profile!

The SAS are so ruthless and so effective that they seem almost like a fictional force of superheroes. The existence of a Japanese comic book called *Master Keaton*, in which the main character is a half-Japanese, half-English insurance investigator who served in the SAS and frequently uses the combat and survival skills he learned there, is a testimony to the fascination that the force exerts on people all around the world.

The SAS was founded in 1941, in Africa, by a young officer called David Stirling. He believed in the need to maximize the element of surprise while minimizing manpower and equipment. He had a force of sixty men which he divided into self-sufficient teams of five, which were each responsible for planning and carrying out its own operations. In North Africa they had notable successes, particularly with attacks on airfields, though Stirling himself was captured and spent two years in captivity.

　SASの隊員選抜試験はむずかしいことで有名で（合格者は20人に1人）、受験できるのはすでに普通部隊に所属している兵士のみである。試験は4週間の耐久テストから始まる。耐久テストに合格したら、次は4ヵ月にわたる訓練が待っている。最後の1ヵ月間は武器の訓練と、食料も充分な衣服も持たずに放りだされて追跡される実践サバイバル・コースに費やされる。晴れて入隊を許されると、世界各地の作戦行動や演習に派遣され、つねに最高水準の技術を身につけておかねばならない。日本のサラリーマンに似て、SASの兵士には私生活などないのである。

　SASの活動の場はおもに北アイルランドに限られていたが、イラン大使館突入で世間の注目を浴びて以降は、フォークランド紛争や湾岸戦争（スカッド・ミサイルを使用不能にした）における敵前線背後の活躍でさらにその名を高めた。一般市民のSASに対する関心はきわめて高く、イラク軍の前線背後におけるSASの偵察行動に関する実話をおさめた『ブラヴォー・ツー・ゼロ』は1994年に出版されて85万部を売り、ジョン・グリシャムの『依頼人』と『シンドラーのリスト』に次いでこの年のベストセラー3位となった。

The selection process for the SAS is notoriously difficult (about one in twenty people get through), and is only open to people who are already serving in the regular army. Selection begins with a four week endurance test. If you pass this, four-months of training will follow. The final month consists of a Combat Survival course—in which you are sent out without food and without adequate clothing and hunted—and weapons training. If accepted into the Service, you are sent on operations and exercises all over the world in order to keep your skills at the highest pitch. SAS people, rather like Japanese salarymen, have no private life!

The SAS were active in Northern Ireland, but after coming to public attention with the storming of the Iranian embassy, their behind-the-lines activities in the Falklands War and the Gulf War (where they disabled Scud missiles) attracted great attention. Such is the interest in the SAS that in 1994 *Bravo Two Zero*, a book which recounted the true story of an SAS patrol behind enemy lines in Iraq, sold 850,000 copies, making it the third best-selling book of the year behind John Grisham's *The Client* and *Schindler's List*.

「英国」おもしろ雑学事典
All You Wanted to Know About the U.K.

1999年5月14日　第1刷発行

著　著　　ジャイルズ・マリー

発行者　　野間佐和子

発行所　　講談社インターナショナル株式会社
　　　　　〒112-8652　東京都文京区音羽1-17-14
　　　　　電話：03-3944-6493（編集部）
　　　　　　　　03-3944-6492（営業部）

印刷所　　大日本印刷株式会社

製本所　　株式会社 堅省堂

講談社バイリンガル・ブックス

1 英語で話す「日本」Q&A / Talking About Japan Q & A 📼

講談社インターナショナル 編　　　　　320ページ　ISBN 4-7700-2026-0

外国の人と話すとき、必ず出てくる話題は「日本」のこと。でも英語力よりも前に困るのは、日本について知らないことがいっぱいという事実です。政治、経済から文化までモヤモヤの知識をスッキリさせてくれる「日本再発見」の書。

2 日米比較 冠婚葬祭のマナー
Do It Right : Japanese & American Social Etiquette

ジェームス・M・バーダマン, 倫子・バーダマン 著　　192ページ　ISBN 4-7700-2025-2

アメリカでは結婚式や葬式はどのように行われるのか？　お祝いや香典は？……そしてアメリカの人たちも、日本の事情を知りたがります。これだけあればもう困らない。日米冠婚葬祭マニュアル、バイリンガル版。

3 英語で折り紙 / Origami in English

山口 真 著　　　　　168ページ　ISBN 4-7700-2027-9

たった一枚の紙から無数の造形が生まれ出る……外国の人たちは、その面白さに目を見張ります。折るとき、英語で説明できるようにバイリンガルにしました。ホームステイ、留学、海外駐在に必携の一冊です。

4 英語で読む日本史 / Japanese History : 11 Experts Reflect on the Past

英文日本大事典 編　　　　　232ページ　ISBN 4-7700-2024-4

11人の超一流ジャパノロジストたちが英語で書き下ろした日本全史。外国人の目から見た日本史はどういうものか、また日本の歴史事項を英語で何と表現するのか。新しい視点が想像力をかき立てます。

5 ベスト・オブ 宮沢賢治短編集 / The Tales of Miyazawa Kenji

宮沢賢治 著　ジョン・ベスター 訳　　216ページ　ISBN 4-7700-2081-3

「注文の多い料理店」「どんぐりと山猫」「祭の晩」「鹿踊りのはじまり」「土神ときつね」「オッベルと象」「毒もみの好きな署長さん」「セロ弾きのゴーシュ」の代表作8編を精選。ジョン・ベスターの名訳でどうぞ。

6 「Japan」クリッピング　ワシントン・ポストが書いた「日本」
Views of Japan from The Washington Post Newsroom

東郷茂彦 著　　　　　264ページ　ISBN 4-7700-2023-6

アメリカの世論をリードするワシントン・ポストに書かれた「Japan」……政治、外交、経済、社会のジャンルで取り上げられた日本の姿を、国際ジャーナリストが解説し、その背後にある問題点を浮き彫りにする一冊。

7 マザー・グース　愛される唄70選
Mother Goose : 70 Nursery Rhymes

谷川俊太郎 訳　渡辺 茂 解説　　　184ページ　ISBN 4-7700-2078-3

「マイ・フェア・レディー」や「お熱いのがお好き」という題名も、マザー・グースからの引用だったってこと、ご存じでしたか？　英米人にとって必須教養であるこの童謡集を、詩人・谷川俊太郎の名訳と共にお楽しみください。

8 ニッポン見聞録 大好きな日本人に贈る新・開国論
Heisei Highs and Lows

トム・リード 著　　　　　　　　　　　224ページ　ISBN 4-7700-2092-9

国際化の進む日本ですが、アメリカのジャーナリストが鋭い目と耳で浮き彫りにした
ニッポンの姿は、驚くほど平穏でいとおしく、恥ずかしいくらい強欲で無知なもので
した。トムが大好きな日本人へ贈る新・開国論。

9 ベスト・オブ 窓ぎわのトットちゃん
Best of Totto-chan : The Little Girl at the Window

黒柳徹子 著　ドロシー・ブリトン 訳　　　　240ページ　ISBN 4-7700-2127-5

小学校一年生にして「退学」になったトットちゃんは、転校先の校長先生に「君は本
当にいい子なんだよ」と温かい言葉のシャワーで励まされます……バイリンガル版で、
あの空前の大ベストセラーの感動をもう一度！

10 銀河鉄道の夜 / Night Train to the Stars

宮沢賢治 著　ジョン・ベスター 訳　　　　184ページ　ISBN 4-7700-2131-3

賢治童話の中でも最も人気の高い「銀河鉄道の夜」は、賢治の宗教心と科学精神が反
映された独特の世界──天空、自然、大地がみごとに描かれ、光と音と動きに満ち溢
れています。ジョバンニと一緒に銀河を旅してみませんか。

11 英語で話す「日本の謎」Q&A 外国人が聞きたがる100のWHY 📼
100 Tough Questions for Japan

板坂 元 監修　　　　　　　　　　　248ページ　ISBN 4-7700-2091-0

なぜ、結婚式は教会で、葬式はお寺でなんてことができるの？　なぜ、大人までがマ
ンガを読むの？　なぜ、時間とお金をかけてお茶を飲む練習をするの？──こんな外
国人の問いをつきつめてゆくと、日本文化の核心が見えてきます。

12 英語で話す「日本の心」 和英辞典では引けないキーワード197
Keys to the Japanese Heart and Soul

英文日本大事典 編　　　　　　　　　328ページ　ISBN 4-7700-2082-1

一流のジャパノロジスト53人が解説した「日本の心」を知るためのキーワード集。
「わび」「さび」「義理人情」「甘え」「根回し」「談合」「みそぎ」など、日本人特有な
「心の動き」を外国人に説明するための強力なツールです。

13 アメリカ日常生活のマナーQ&A / Do As Americans Do

ジェームス・M・バーダマン, 倫子・バーダマン 著　264ページ　ISBN 4-7700-2128-3

"How do you do?" に "How do you do?" と答えてはいけないということ、ご存知でし
たか？　日本では当たり前と思われていたことがマナー違反だったのです。旅行で、
駐在で、留学でアメリカに行く人必携のマナー集。

14 ニッポン不思議発見！ 日本文化を英語で語る50の名エッセイ集
Discover Japan: Words, Customs and Concepts

日本文化研究所 編　松本道弘 訳　　　　272ページ　ISBN 4-7700-2142-9

絶望的な場合ですら、日本人は「そこをなんとか」という言葉を使って、相手に甘え
ようとする……こんな指摘をうけると、いかに日本人は独特なものの考え方をしてい
るか分かります。あなたも「不思議」を発見してみませんか。

15 英語で日本料理 / 100 Recipes from Japanese Cooking

辻調理師専門学校　畑耕一郎, 近藤一樹 著
272ページ　（カラー口絵16ページ）　ISBN 4-7700-2079-1

外国の人と親しくなる最高の手段は、日本料理を作ってあげること、そしてその作り方を教えてあげることです。代表的な日本料理100品の作り方を、外国の計量法も入れながら、バイリンガルで分かりやすく説明します。

16 まんが 日本昔ばなし / Once Upon a Time in Japan

川内彩友美 編　ラルフ・マッカーシー 訳
160ページ　ISBN 4-7700-2173-9

人気テレビシリーズ「まんが日本昔ばなし」から、「桃太郎」「金太郎」「一寸法師」など、より抜きの名作8話をラルフ・マッカーシーの名訳でお届けします。ホームステイなどでも役に立つ一冊です。

17 イラスト 日本まるごと事典 / Japan at a Glance

インターナショナル・インターンシップ・プログラムス 著
256ページ　（2色刷）　ISBN 4-7700-2080-5

1000点以上のイラストを使って日本のすべてを紹介──自然、文化、社会はもちろんのこと、折り紙の折り方、着物の着方から、ナベで米を炊く方法や「あっちむいてホイ」の遊び方まで国際交流に必要な知識とノウハウを満載。

18 ビジュアル 英語で読む日本国憲法 / The Constitution of Japan

英文日本大百科事典 編
208ページ　ISBN 4-7700-2191-7

難しいと思っていた「日本国憲法」も、英語で読むと不思議とよく分かります。日本国憲法を、59点の写真を使って、バイリンガルで分かりやすく解説しました。条文中に出てくる難解な日本語には、ルビや説明がついています。

19 英語で話す「世界」Q&A / Talking About the World Q & A

講談社インターナショナル 編
320ページ　ISBN 4-7700-2006-6

今、世界にはいくつの国家があるか、ご存じですか？　対立をはらみながらも、急速に1つの運命共同体になっていく「世界」──外国の人と話すとき知らなければならない「世界」に関する国際人必携の「常識集」です。

20 誤解される日本人　外国人がとまどう41の疑問
The Inscrutable Japanese

メリディアン・リソーシス・アソシエイツ 編　賀川 洋 著
232ページ　ISBN 4-7700-2129-1

あなたのちょっとした仕草や表情が大きな誤解を招いているかもしれません。「日本人はどんなときに誤解を受けるのか？」そのメカニズムを解説し、「どのように外国人に説明すればよいか」最善の解決策を披露します。

21 英語で話す「アメリカ」Q&A / Talking About the USA Q & A

賀川 洋 著
312ページ　ISBN 4-7700-2005-8

仕事でも留学でも遊びでも、アメリカ人と交際するとき、知っておくと役に立つ「アメリカ小事典」。アメリカ人の精神と社会システムにポイントをおいた解説により、自然、歴史、政治、文化、そして人をバイリンガルで紹介します。

22 英語で話す「日本の文化」/ Japan as I See It

NHK国際放送局文化プロジェクト 編　ダン・ケニー 訳　　208ページ　ISBN 4-7700-2197-6

金田一春彦、遠藤周作、梅原猛、平川祐弘、西堀栄三郎、鯖田豊之、野村万作、井上靖、小松左京、中根千枝の１０人が、日本文化の「謎」を解く。NHKの国際放送で２１の言語で放送され、分かりやすいと世界中で大好評。

23 ベスト・オブ・天声人語 / VOX POPULI, VOX DEI

朝日新聞論説委員室 著　朝日イブニングニュース 訳　　288ページ　ISBN 4-7700-2166-6

「天声人語」は「朝日新聞」の名コラムというよりも、日本を代表するコラムです。香港返還、アムラー現象、たまごっち、マザー・テレサの死など、現代を読み解く傑作56編を、社会・世相、政治、スポーツなどのジャンル別に収録しました。

24 英語で話す「仏教」Q & A / Talking About Buddhism Q & A

高田佳人 著　ジェームス・M・バーダマン 訳　　240ページ　ISBN 4-7700-2161-5

四十九日までに7回も法事をするのは、「亡くなった人が7回受ける裁判をこの世から応援するため」だということ、ご存じでしたか？　これだけは知っておきたい「仏教」に関することがらを、やさしい英語で説明できるようにした入門書です。

25 日本を創った100人 / 100 Japanese You Should Know

板坂 元 監修　英文日本大事典 編　　240ページ　ISBN 4-7700-2159-3

混沌と激動を乗り越え築き上げられた現在の日本。その長い歴史の節目節目で大きな役割を果たした歴史上のキーパーソン100人を、超一流のジャパノロジストたちが解説。グローバルな大競争時代を迎えた今、彼らの生き方が大きな指針となります。

26 NHK「ニュースのキーワード」 NHK: Key Words in the News

NHK国際放送局「ニュースのキーワード」プロジェクト 編　　232ページ　ISBN 4-7700-2342-1

日本で話題になっている時事問題を解説する、NHK国際放送の番組「ニュースのキーワード」から「総会屋」「日本版ビッグバン」「ダイオキシン」など、33のキーワードを収録しました。国際的観点からの解説が、現代の日本の姿を浮き彫りにします。

27 ドタンバのマナー / The Ultimate Guide to Etiquette in Japan

サトウサンペイ 著　　240ページ（オールカラー）　ISBN 4-7700-2193-3

サンペイ流家元が自らしでかした「日常のヘマ」「海外でのヘマ」を一目で分かるようにマンガにした、フレッシュマンに贈る究極のマナー集。新社会人必読！知っていればすむことなのに、知らないために嫌われたり、憎まれてはかないません。

28 茶の本 / The Book of Tea

岡倉天心 著　千 宗室 序と跋　浅野 晃 訳　　264ページ　ISBN 4-7700-2379-0

一碗の茶をすする、そのささやかで簡潔な行為の中に、偉大な精神が宿っている――茶道によせて、日本と東洋の精神文化の素晴らしさを明かし、アジアの理想が回復されることを英文で呼びかけた本書は、日本の心を英語で明かす不朽の名著。

29 まんが 日本昔ばなし 妖しのお話
Once Upon a Time in *Ghostly* Japan

川内彩友美 編　ラルフ・マッカーシー 訳　　　　152ページ　ISBN 4-7700-2347-2

妖しく、怖く、心に響く昔ばなしの名作を英語で読む。人気テレビシリーズ「まんが日本昔ばなし」から、「鶴の恩返し」「雪女」「舌切り雀」「耳なし芳一」「分福茶釜」など8話を収録しました。

30 武士道 / BUSHIDO

新渡戸稲造 著　須知徳平 訳　　　　312ページ　ISBN 4-7700-2402-9

「日本が生んだ最大の国際人」新渡戸博士が英語で著した世界的名著。「日本の精神文化を知る最良の書」として世界17ヵ国語に翻訳され、1世紀にわたって読みつがれてきた不滅の日本人論。国際人必読の1冊。

31 開国ノススメ　孤立化するニッポンへの問題提起 / Open up, Japan!

アンドリュー・ホルバート 著　　　　208ページ　ISBN 4-7700-2348-0

欧米の高級紙誌で活躍する一流の国際ジャーナリストが、海外で問われることの多い、日本の政治・経済・社会システムの問題について「どのように説明すればよいか」のヒントを与えてくれます。

32 NHK「日本ひとくち歳時記」 / Around the Year in Japan

NHK国際放送局「日本一口事典」プロジェクト 編　　　　256ページ　ISBN 4-7700-2457-6

ひな祭り、七夕、運動会、年賀状など季節感あふれる32のキーワードから、日本文化を斬新な視点で、簡潔に分かりやすく解説します。21ヵ国語で放送中のNHK国際放送局が発見した「ニッポン」。

33 「縮み」志向の日本人 / Smaller is Better

李 御寧 著　　　　200ページ　ISBN 4-7700-2445-2

一寸法師から、盆栽、箱庭、茶室、俳句にいたるまで、常に小さいものを求め、小さいものへ向かう「縮み志向」。言語・風俗・文化などが似ており、また日本文化にも影響を与えた韓国、その初代文化大臣を務めた著者によって発見された日本文化の本質。

34 イラスト 日米ジェスチャー事典
The Illustrated Handbook of American and Japanese Gestures

スティーブン・N・ウイリアムス 著　　　　264ページ　ISBN 4-7700-2344-8

知らなかったではすまされない――。誤解を受け、国際問題や大騒動を引き起こしかねない、日本とアメリカのジェスチャーの違いを、ひと目で分かるイラストで解説します。言葉よりモノをいう780のジェスチャー。

35 英語で話す「雑学ニッポン」Q&A / Japan Trivia

素朴な疑問探究会 編　　　　272ページ　ISBN 4-7700-2361-8

日本にいる外国人と飲んでいて、一番盛りあがる話はなんといっても、「ニッポンの謎」についての雑学です。「日本の女性は、なぜ下唇から口紅を塗るの？」「なぜ"鈴木"という名字が多いの？」など、外国人が疑問に思う「なぜ？」に答えます。

講談社バイリンガル・ブックス （オン・カセット）　英語で聞いても面白い！

印のタイトルは、英文テキスト部分を録音したカセット・テープが発売されています。
本との併用により聞く力・話す力を高め、実用的な英語が身につく格好のリスニング教材です。